"Facts are stubborn things."

John Adams

Sermons We See by Edgar Guest

I'd rather see a sermon than hear one any day;
I'd rather one should walk with me than merely
tell the way.
The eye's a better pupil and more willing than
the ear,
Fine counsel is confusing, but example's always
clear;
And the best of all the preachers are the men who
live their creeds,
For to see good put in action is what everybody
needs.
I soon can learn to do it if you'll let me see it
done;
I can watch your hands in action, but your
tongue too fast may run.
And the lecture you deliver may be very wise
and true,
But I'd rather get my lessons by observing what
you do;
For I might misunderstand you and the high
advise you give,
But there's no misunderstanding how you act
and how you live.
When I see a deed of kindness, I am eager to be
kind.
When a weaker brother stumbles and a strong
man stays behind
Just to see if he can help him, then the wish
grows strong in me
To become as big and thoughtful as I know that
friend to be.

And all travelers can witness that the best of guides today
Is not the one who tells them, but the one who shows the way.
One good man teaches many, men believe what they behold;
One deed of kindness noticed is worth forty that are told.
Who stands with men of honor learns to hold his honor dear,
For right living speaks a language which to every one is clear.
Though an able speaker charms me with his eloquence, I say,
I'd rather see a sermon than to hear one, any day.*

These pages present portions of our history in black and white. Justice Oliver Wendell Holmes intoned that "A page of history is worth a pound of logic." By looking *Ad Fontes* (at the sources) and not imagining our past full of fluid possibilities we discover, in our documented history, *multum in parvo* (much in little). Each one a sermon to see as it were not overly preachy, but a testimony to a time and place where in America we were naturally going to give honor where honor was due.

This poem is in the public domain.

Our Stamp of Approval

This book started from observations, conversations and memories with good friends who share an appreciation for the uniqueness and exceptional history we have as Americans.

In the process of production I referenced other sources, specifically *Stamping our Heritage* by Davidson & Diamant and *An American History Album- the Story of the United States told through Stamps* by Worek & Worek and a number of websites, specifically The US Postal Museum to supplement the content.

Cover design: Bill Fortenberry

Vox audita perit littera scripta manet

"The heard voice perishes, but the written letter remains."

Deuteronomy 4:32 "For ask now of the days that are past ...whether there hath been any such thing as this great thing is, or hath been heard like it?"

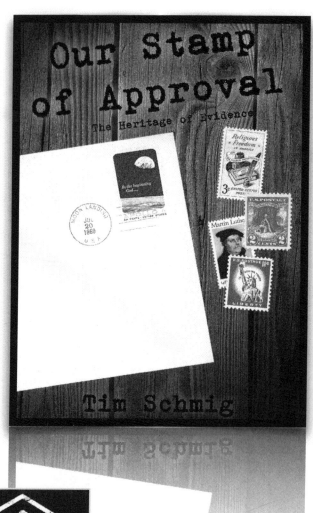

Tim Schmig
BA, MM, D. Litt

This story started, like all stories do, with very humble beginnings. In the early 1990's I started to visit Washington, DC on a regular basis and from that this has grown in to presentations and tours of our Nation's Capitol. My first book Stories in Stones The Heritage of Evidence in our National Monuments sent me on the path asking 'I wonder where else we can find remnants of our godly heritage?' This little book is designed to serve as a starting point for all of those out there to begin their own quest to discover the truth that we as a Nation have hid in plain sight.

Most of these photographs are in public domain. Experience has shown me that to include a website address to credit a source is often frustrating for the reader as links go away or are rewritten and useless to the reader. There is no attempt on my part to not rightfully credit anyone.

DEDICATION

To Hannah, our stamp collector,
who taught us that big messages
can be seen in small places.

To Rebekah, who taught me
to teach others with compassion.

To Sarah,
who sees big potential in
little people every day.

Oh that my words were
now written! Oh that they
were printed in a book!

Job 19:23

The truth is important, sadly, most miss it.
This book will be like a parable. Some will look at it and say to themselves, how could anyone possibly miss this? It is so obvious. Others will give the usual dismissive, "yeah but what about..." and change the subject as rapidly as possible. I acknowledge that as a nation, we are not perfect, far from it. Yet, on the scale of human history we are exceptional. I challenge anyone to find a nation that so freely embraced the tenets of Christianity and distinctly planned them front and center for all to see. To every committee, architect, designer, artist and draftsman who ever had the courage to propose and implement the historic seals and designs, I acknowledge my debt of gratitude.

IN GOD WE TRUST
first appeared on the 1864 two-cent coin.

9

"... A bit of paper just large enough to bear the stamp, and covered at the back with a glutinous wash"

This was the first mention by Rowland Hill of what became the world's first adhesive postage stamp. He was answering the questions of a parliamentary enquiry into the Post Office in February 1837 shortly after the publication of his pamphlet *Post Office reform; Its Importance and Practicality.*

In this pamphlet Hill had challenged the high, extremely complex and anomalous postal rates then in force. He suggested a low uniform rate of postage based on weight and prepaid. At this time the high rates were based on distance and the number of sheets in a letter, and normally they were paid by the recipient. Many letters were also carried free.

https://www.postalmuseum.org/collections/penny-black/

The famous "Inverted Jenny" stamp. The mistake is that the plane is flying upside down. Issued on May 10, 1918 it is the most famous example of a mistaken printed stamp. Using a two press process the red color is printed, and then the blue is printed on the second pass. Mistakes happened on other two press stamps in the past and most of these sheets were destroyed by the postal engravers. One sheet of 100 made it past the inspectors and was sold at a U.S. Post office to William Roby and the Inverted Jenny entered American legend and lore.

In 2016 one inverted Jenny sold at auction for $1,175,00.00.

The United States Code at 36 U.S.C. § 302 states: 'In God we Trust' is the national motto. The 84th Congress passed a joint resolution unanimously and without debate "declaring IN GOD WE TRUST the national motto of the United States." The law was signed by President Eisenhower on July 30, 1956."

The first stamp issues were authorized
by an act of Congress and
approved on March 3, 1847.

This collection of U.S. Postage stamps and
other seals, charters, and images shows us
that big messages in small spaces are no
accident. Planning, preparation, and
presentation are meticulously guided through
committees and debated before ever granted
final approval enabling telling of the biggest
story in the smallest space.

Matthew 13:13 "Because they seeing
see not, and hearing they
hear not, neither do they
understand"

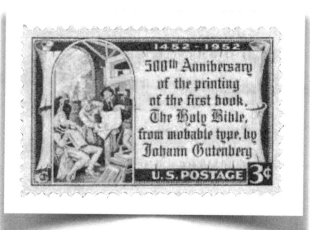

Arguably the most influential invention of the Millennium, the first book printed on the movable type printing press was a Bible. Since then, the Bible has been universally acclaimed best-seller and in more homes and hearts than any other book in the world.

"Observe the hand of God in the wise and beneficent timing of events in the dawn of our history. The events of history are not accidents".

Pastor S.W. Foljambe

Martin Luther

1483-1983 USA 20c

"So quickly were Luther's pamphlets set in type, printed, duplicated and sold, that Luther said it was as if Angels were his couriers, so rapidly were his words dispensed throughout the realm."

Dr. Ed Panosian

The Bishop's Bible [1572, 1602] commenting on Psalm 45:9 "Ophir is thought to be the land in the West Coast, of late found by Christopher Colombo: from whence this day is brought most fine Gold."

(Excerpts from) America Is Hard to See

Columbus may have worked the wind

And with the gold in hand to show for

His claim it was another Ophir.

Had but Columbus known enough

He might have boldly made the bluff

That better than Da Gama's gold
He had been given to behold

The race's future trial place,
A fresh start for the human race.

America is hard to see.
Less partial witnesses than he
In book on book have testified
They could not see it from outside—

Or inside either for that matter.

Robert Frost 1951

And ye shall hallow the fiftieth year, and *proclaim liberty throughout all the land* unto all the inhabitants thereof: it shall be a jubilee unto you; and ye shall return every man unto his possession, and ye shall return every man unto his family.

Leviticus 25:10

Moslem pirates prevented a safe passage for merchants and traders through the Mediterranean so Christopher Columbus searched for a trade route to the far east.

Our history is one of a New World, not just and Old World in a new place. President Benjamin Harrison encouraged Americans to give thanks for "Divine Providence for the devout faith of the discoverer, and for the Divine care and guidance which has directed our history and so abundantly blessed our people."

Since these clear cogent words of reflection on the importance of the discoverer, Christopher Columbus has become an empty vessel for every aggrieved party to pour their prejudice and interpretations of his value to American History. In 1892 America celebrated his life with two different postage stamps.

Almost forgotten in early American history is Reverend Richard Hakluyt's influence on the proper balance between economic interests and the spiritual emphasis to colonize this vast wilderness of North America.

Early attempts to extract economic gain failed routinely. Instructions by financiers to search for gold and silver along the coast of Virginia led to precious time lost in establishing communities growing necessary crops. Even by 1691, a group of Virginians commissioned Dr. James Blair to sail to London to raise funds for the emerging College of William and Mary, for the training of men for the ministry.

Fortunately, Reverend Hakluyt's influence in motivating settlers are recorded in his 1584 treatise *A Discourse Concerning Western Planting* presented to Queen Elizabeth. "We shall by planting there enlarge the glory of the gospel, and from England plant sincere religion, and provide a safe and a sure place to receive people from all parts of the world that are forced to flee for the truth of God's word."

To say that the Pilgrims disagreed with the rites of the Church of England would be an understatement. They did not desire to stay in England and purify the church from within. They desired separation and thought of themselves as separatists.

They would not object to themselves being referred to as Pilgrims as they embraced the term as found in I Peter 2:11 *Dearly beloved I beseech you as strangers and pilgrims abstain from fleshly lusts which war against the soul.*

To get to the new World they used their connections among the Virginia Company placing themselves in indentured servitude for seven years to work and send goods and profits back to England in exchange for their charter and vessels to carry them over the Atlantic Ocean to a land of new opportunities and freedom from the oppressive Church of England.

They departed September 16, 1620 on the *Mayflower* arriving after a voyage that was nerve wracking in length coupled with below deck confinement during rough seas and the peril of the ships mast breaking mid voyage. They arrived with the loss of only one life onboard, that of a "blasphemous' ships mate lost at sea.

"The Lord will be our God and will delight to dwell among us as His one people."

"For we must consider that we shall be as a city upon a hill, the eyes of all people are upon us."
Puritan Governor John Winthrop

"The Reformation was preceded by the discovery of America as if the Almighty graciously meant to open a sanctuary to the persecuted in future years when home should afford neither friendship nor safety."
Thomas Paine   *Common Sense* 1776

The pilgrims, as we call them, were known known by their peers as "Precisionists" in that they precisely desired certain religious practices to be observed. They were not impressed with the official Church of England with its Book of Common Prayer and regulated church services or the observance of religious holidays like Christmas on December 25 or the wearing of jewelry or makeup on women. Their leaders left England for Holland to avoid that knock at the door in the night by the local officials, but soon found life in Holland just as intolerable especially for their children.

They settled on the idea of transplanting themselves to the New World, to be left alone to practice their faith. Their departing was not going to missed by their fellow Englishmen who regarded them as "psalm singing religious nuts with guns". Realizing they we not in Virginia when they landed, as was the plan, they put in writing the first document of government by consent of the governed. It begins with a prayer.

In the name of God, Amen… Undertaken for the glory of God and the advancement of the Christian Faith

They were going to make society right, bring it back to the beginning to its uncorrupted pure origins of the Bible Alone, by Faith Alone, with Grace Alone, Through Christ Alone, For God's Glory Alone.

Yet we may not look at great things here. It is enough that we shall have Heaven, though we should pass through Hell to it. We here enjoy God and Jesus Christ. Is not this enough? What would we have more? I thank God; I like so well to be here as I do not repent my coming and if I were to come again.

John Winthrop Pilgrim leader to his wife Margaret back in England 1631.

"South America was settled by the Spanish who went there in search of gold. North America was settled by the Pilgrims who went there in search of God."

Quoting the President of Argentina, Robert Babson in his *Fundamentals of Prosperity* (1921)

The settlement of America had its origins in the unsettlement of Europe. Lewis Mumford
The Golden Day 1926

Hebrews 11:13 These all died in faith… and confessed that they were strangers and pilgrims on the earth.

Mayflower Compact

In the name of God, Amen. We, whose names are underwritten, the loyal subjects of our dread Sovereigne Lord, King James, by the grace of God, of Great Britaine, France and Ireland king, defender of the faith, etc. having undertaken, for the glory of God, and advancement of the Christian faith, and honour of our king and country, a voyage to plant the first colony in the Northerne parts of Virginia, do by these presents solemnly and mutually in the presence of God and one of another, covenant and combine ourselves together into a civil body politick, for our better ordering and preservation, and furtherance of the ends aforesaid; and by virtue hereof to enact, constitute, and frame such just and equal laws, ordinances, acts, constitutions and offices, from time to time, as shall be thought most meete and convenient for the general good of the Colonie unto which we promise all due submission and obedience. In witness whereof we have hereunder subscribed our names at Cape-Cod the 11. of November, in the year of the reign of our sovereign lord, King James, of England, France and Ireland, the eighteenth, and of Scotland the fifty-fourth.   Anno Dom. 1620.

While the Pilgrims imagined for themselves a "city on a hill" they sought religious tolerance for themselves that they were unwilling to bestow on others. One example was Roger Williams, a religious Puritan who placed a value on his Liberty of Conscience. The 1636-1936 passage stamp of Roger Williams has him holding a book or tablet with the words *Soul Liberty* engraved on the front.

Williams did not believe that the civil magistrates in Massachusetts should be enforcing the laws on the first tablet of Moses. These commandments dealt with the Lord's prohibitions of blasphemy and honoring the sabbath among other things.

Banishment led to his wilderness journey through the woods of New England for his heretical beliefs, in the eyes of the General Court of Massachusetts Bay Colony. He purchased land from the Narragansset Indian Chiefs. His beliefs compelled him purchase land from the natives rather than acquisition though confiscation. Soon other exiles followed him to the colony of Rhode Island, mockingly referred to as Rogue Island by the those in Massachusetts.

The guiding principle of Roger Williams towards religious expressions was that of liberty and toleration even extending it to Jews and Quakers in Rhode Island. In 1663 a royal charter for his colony was granted from Charles II.

An early abolitionist, advocate of separation of church and state and defender of liberty of conscience believing "that no one should be compelled to worship in violation of their conscience."
The Rhode Island Charter has clear indications of honoring Christian civil origins overtones.

Acts 24:16 Herein do I exercise myself, to have always a conscience void of offense toward God, and toward man.

Roger William's famous 'Ship' letter making
the case for religious liberty and liberty of
conscience

1655

To the Town of Providence,

That ever I should speak or write a tittle, that
tends to such an infinite liberty of conscience,
is a mistake, and which I have ever disclaimed
and abhorred. To prevent such mistakes, I shall
at present only propose this case: There goes
many a ship to sea, with many hundred souls
in one ship, whose weal and woe is common,
and is a true picture of a commonwealth, or a
human combination or society. It hath fallen
out sometimes, that both Papists and
Protestants, Jews and Turks, may be embarked
in one ship; upon which supposal I affirm, that
all the liberty of conscience, that ever I
pleaded for, turns upon these two hinges--that
none of the Papists, Protestants, Jews, or Turks
be forced to come to the ship's prayers or
worship, nor compelled from their own
particular prayers or worship, if they practice
any. I further add, that I never denied, that
notwithstanding this liberty, the commander of
this ship ought to command the ship's course,
yea, and also command that

justice, peace, and sobriety be kept and practiced, both among the seamen and all the passengers. If any of the seamen refuse to perform their services, or passengers to pass their freight; if any refuse to help, in person or purse, towards the common charges or defense; if any refuse to obey the common laws and orders of the ship, concerning their common peace or preservation; if any shall mutiny and rise up against their commanders and officers; if any should preach or write that there ought to be no commanders or officers, because all are equal in Christ, therefore no masters nor officers, no laws or orders, nor corrections nor punishments; I say, I never denied, but in such cases, whatever is pretended, the commander or commanders may judge, resist, compel, and punish such transgressors, according to their deserts and merits. This if seriously and honestly minded, may, if it so please the Father of Lights, let in some light to such as willingly shut not their eyes.

I remain studious of your common peace and liberty.

A disappointment to his Father and namesake, the younger Penn, a Quaker convert, desired to set up a utopian community for a "Holy Experiment" similar to the efforts of the Pilgrims in Massachusetts Bay.

Mindful of Roger Williams colony in Rhode Island, he tried to model Pennsylvania - (Penn's Woods) after religious tolerance and cordial relations with the natives. His first city was Philadelphia, named after the Biblical city being laid out with wide expansive streets as to invite openness and community. Philadelphia, the "City of Brotherly Love"would be his 'great town' in his charter colony of 48,00 square miles between New York and Maryland.

The first Seal of the Commonwealth of Massachusetts 1629-1686. A Native American Indian holding an arrow pointed down in a gesture of peace and the words, "Come over and help us," taken from the Bible Acts 16:9 emphasizing the missionary aspirations of the original colonists.

The original motto,
"Truth (Veritas) for Christ (Christo) and the
Church (Ecclesiae)," was adopted in 1692 and
was a part of their original seal.

Modern day seal of Harvard
Truth for Christ and the Church is removed.

If any gentleman supposes this controversy [Tea Tax] to be nothing to the present purpose [the gathering storm], he is grossly mistaken. It spread an universal alarm against the authority of Parliament. It excited a general and just apprehension, that bishops, and dioceses, and churches, and priests, and tithes, were to be imposed on us by Parliament. It was known

that neither king, nor ministry, nor archbishops, could appoint bishops in America, without an act of Parliament; and if Parliament could tax us, they could establish the Church of England, with all its creeds, articles, tests, ceremonies, and tithes, and prohibit all other churches, as conventicles and schism shops.
John Adams to H. Niles, 13 February 1818

"Death is more eligible than slavery. A free-born people are not required by the religion of Christ to submit to tyranny, but may make use of such power as God has given them to recover and support their...liberties."
Commenting on the Boston Tea Party, the men of Marlborough, MA unanimously proclaimed in
January 1773.

The most remembered line of his famous speech at St. John's Church in Richmond, Virginia on March 23, 1775 at the Second Meeting of the Virginia Convention, the clarion words of "Give me Liberty or give me Death" defined the passion of Patrick Henry.

However, it is the paragraphs leading up to this crescendo that merits just as much attention to know the heart of Patrick Henry.

"They tell us, sir, that we are weak—unable to cope with so formidable an adversary. But when shall we be stronger? Will it be the next week, or the next year? Will it be when we are totally disarmed, and when a British guard shall be stationed in every house? Shall we gather strength by irresolution and inaction? Shall we acquire the means of effectual resistance by lying supinely on our backs and hugging the delusive phantom of hope, until our enemies shall have bound us hand and foot?

Sir, we are not weak if we make a proper use of those means which the God of nature has placed in our power. Three millions of people armed in the holy cause of liberty, and in such a country as that which we possess, are invincible by any force which our enemy can send against us. Besides, air, we shall not fight our battles alone. There is a just God who presides over the destinies of nations, and who will raise up friends to fight our battles for us. The battle, sir, is not to the strong alone; it is to the vigilant, the active, the brave. Besides, sir, we have no election. If we were base enough to desire it, it is now too late to retire from the contest. There is no

retreat but in submission and slavery! Our chains are forged! Their clanking may be heard on the plains of Boston! The war is inevitable—and let is come! I repeat it, sir, let it come!

9

It is in vain, sir, to extenuate the matter. Gentlemen may cry, Peace, Peace—but there is no peace. The war is actually begun! The next gale that sweeps from the north will bring to our ears the clash of resounding arms! Our brethren are already in the field! Why stand we here idle? What is it that gentlemen wish? What would they have? Is life so dear, or peace so sweet, as to be purchased at the price of chains and slavery? Forbid it, Almighty God! I know not what course others may take; but as for me, give me liberty or give me death!

The life of Patrick Henry is an example that Americans will stand up to tyranny and in keeping with our founding principles we are not afraid to say "I disagree" in the face of over-reaching magistrates.

Religious freedom and liberty of Conscience gives us the right to worship as we please, in the church of our choice according to the dictates of our conscience.

In 1637 the present Town of Flushing, New York was a Dutch Colony and the petition was the first to give voice to the basic American principle that we should all be free to worship without government coercion. Standing up for the minority of Quakers in the town, the authors voiced a fundamental right that would become part of our first Amendment sending the Remonstrance to their Dutch Governor even though it was of no real benefit to themselves.

In 1775 Fort Ticonderoga was known as the Gibraltar of America and highly respected as the Gateway to the Continent. Colonial forces believed its capture to be of interest both militarily and for the morale of the Colonial cause. In the early morning hours of May 10, 1775 with sword raised Ethan Allen approached the commander in charge of the fort, and demanded he "Surrender this fort instantly." "By what authority" the commander inquired. "In the name of the great Jehovah and the Continental Army" Allen replied. Fort Ticonderoga was surrendered without loss of life.

Later, the guns from Fort Ticonderoga were the ones used during the assault on the British ships in Boston Harbor, Colonel Knox and his men transported them over 300 hundred miles overland to Dorchester Heights overlooking the harbor and the bombardment for this heightened vantage point convinced the British ships to withdraw from their cannon range and relocate to New York City.

We appreciate our national symbols whether it is the Betsy Ross flag, showing a new constellation of stars in the political universe, the Majestic Eagle or the Liberty Bell, they all have a place of reverence in our hearts. The bell was a gift to the people of Pennsylvania in 1751 on the 50th anniversary of the colony. "Proclaim Liberty throughout all the land unto all the inhabitants thereof" Leviticus 25:10 emblazoned along the shoulder of the bell.

Celebrating the 150th anniversary an exposition was held in the city of Philadelphia. A postage stamp commemorates the giant replica above the road leading to the Liberty Bell grounds. Motorcades passed under the replica as part of the national festivities.

In this hour of darkness and of danger, when 'foes were strong and friends were few,' when every human prospect presented to the commander at Valley Forge was disheartening, he retires to a sequestered spot, and there laid the cause of his bleeding country at the throne of grace. That country had appealed in vain to the justice of her acknowledged sovereign; he pleads her cause before the King of Kings. He sought to link our cause, by a sincere devotion, to the immutable throne of justice; to find wisdom to guide his own action; to place the country in the right, so that he might bring upon her prosperity, as the natural result of justice to the injured.

How full of interest is this scene! How instructive! How sublime! Let our children come up from their cradles through the remotest generations to contemplate this picture. Let parents open it to their admiring families. Let it be hung on the parlor walls, ornament the center tables, be pictured on the tapestry, be grouped with every cradle scene, recited in every nursery, that it may meet the early vision, and affect the young heart of every child who may breathe the free air of this land of freedom—'Washington is at prayer.' Well did he earn the title of 'patriarch'—'the father of his country.' As we honor him, and teach our children to give him honor, may we also love and honor, and teach our children to acknowledge the God of our fathers, who alone giveth the victory.

The Family Circle—1847

"We remember the picture of the Father of our Country, on his knees at Valley Forge seeking divine guidance in the cold gloom of a bitter winter. Thus Washington gained strength to lead to independence a nation dedicated to the belief that each of us is divinely endowed with indestructible rights."

February 7, 1954 President Dwight Eisenhower's broadcast from the White House for the American Legion's Back-to-God Program.

The title page of Noah Webster's Blue Back Speller contained this gem of instruction: "Begin with infant in the cradle, let the first word he lisps be Washington."

George Washington's Will designating his battle swords to his nephews: "These swords are accompanied with and injunction not to unsheathe them for the purpose of shedding blood, except in self defense, or in the defense of their Country and its rights; and in the latter case, to keep them unsheathed, and prefer falling on them in their hands, to the relinquishment thereof..."

"George Washington is perhaps the purest and noblest Character of modern times." The Duke of Wellington, Briton's foremost soldier and the victor at Waterloo.

Treaty of Paris 1783
US Bicentennial 20 cents

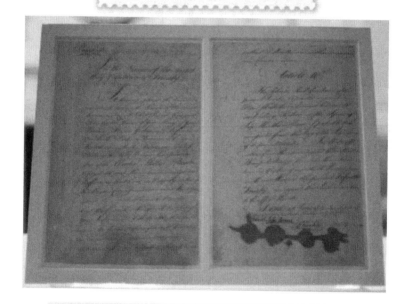

Preamble:

In the Name of the most Holy and Undivided Trinity

Signed Ben Franklin, John Adams &
John Jay
Conclusion: Done at Paris, this third day
of September in the year of our Lord,
one thousand seven hundred and
eighty-three.

Ben Franklin at the Constitutional Convention.

Mr. President

The small progress we have made after 4 or five weeks close attendance & continual reasonings with each other-our different sentiments on almost every question, several of the last producing as many noes as ays, is methinks a melancholy proof of the imperfection of the Human

Understanding. We indeed seem to feel our own want of political wisdom, since we have been running about in search of it. We have gone back to ancient history for models of Government, and examined the different forms of those Republics which having been formed with the seeds of their own dissolution now no longer exist. And we have viewed Modern States all round Europe, but find none of their Constitutions suitable to our circumstances.

In this situation of this Assembly, groping as it were in the dark to find political truth, and scarce able to distinguish it when presented to us, how has it happened, Sir, that we have not hitherto once thought of humbly applying to the Father of lights to illuminate our understandings? In the beginning of the Contest with G. Britain, when we were sensible of danger we had daily prayer in this room for the divine protection.- Our prayers, Sir, were heard, & they were graciously answered. All of us who were engaged in the struggle must have observed frequent instances of a superintending providence in our favor.

I have lived, Sir, a long time, and the longer I live, the more convincing proofs I see of this truth- that God Governs in the affairs of men. And if a sparrow cannot fall to the ground without his notice, is it probable that an empire can rise without his aid?

To that kind providence we owe this happy opportunity of consulting in peace on the means of establishing our future national felicity. And have we now forgotten that powerful friend? or do we imagine that we no longer need his assistance? I have lived, Sir, a long time, and the longer I live, the more convincing proofs I see of this truth- that God Governs in the affairs of men. And if a sparrow cannot fall to the ground without his notice, is it probable that an empire can rise without his aid? We have been assured, Sir, in the sacred writings, that "except the Lord build the House they labour in vain that build it." I firmly believe this; and I also believe that without his concurring aid we shall succeed in this political building no better, than the Builders of Babel: We shall be divided by our little partial local interests; our projects will be confounded, and we ourselves shall become a reproach and bye word down to future ages. And what is worse, mankind may hereafter from this unfortunate instance, despair of establishing Governments by Human wisdom and leave it to chance, war and conquest. *

* Doctor Franklin's noble request for a local minister to lead in prayer failed to pass as discussions broke down as to how this minister was to be paid.

Moses, standing on the shore and extending his hand over the sea thereby causing the same to overwhelm Pharaoh who is sitting in an open chariot a crown on his head and a sword in his hand raised from the pillar of cloud and fire reaching to Moses to express that he acts by command of the deity motto 'Rebellion To Tyrants Is Obedience To God.'

Ben Franklin Statesman, Printer, Inventor
Describing his proposal for the great seal of the United States 1776

Franklin and the others believed that what they experienced in the fight for Independence was nothing short of God's miraculous providence and thus reminiscent of Israel's deliverance from the Egyptian Army at the Red Sea.

"I do solemnly swear (or affirm) that I will faithfully execute the Office of President of the United States, and will to the best of my Ability, preserve, protect and defend the Constitution of the United States."

Presidents since Washington spontaneously add "So Help Me God" to their Oath of Office.

This is a paraphrase of one of the Founder's most often quoted verses:
Micah 6:8 He hath shewed thee, O man what is good; and what doth the Lord require of thee, but to do justly, and to love mercy and to walk humbly with thy God?

Star Spangled Banner 3rd Stanza

O thus be it ever, when freemen shall stand
Between their loved homes and the war's desolation.
Blest with vict'ry and peace, may the Heav'n rescued land
Praise the Power that hath made and preserved us a nation!
Then conquer we must, when our cause it is just,
And this be our motto: 'In God is our trust.'
And the star-spangled banner in triumph shall wave
O'er the land of the free and the home of the brave!

Earliest Surviving copy of the
Star Spangled Banner 1814

And this be our Motto, in God is our Trust sums up the clear connection between a nations' trust and faith in God and the blessings both temporal and lasting that flow from an unashamed belief that God governs in the affairs of men and the principles of God blessing those that bless Him and curses those that curse Him.

Blessed is the nation whose God is the Lord. Psalm

One of the two large paintings in the House of Representatives is of George Washington, the other is Lafayette. Why such a prominent position and high honor for someone who was not an American? In addition to being a favorite General of Revolution, Lafayette returned to America 1824-25. After receiving many honors, including laying the cornerstone on the Bunker Hill Monument, when asked what gift America could bestow upon him Lafayette requested two barrels of soil from Bunker Hill to take with him and later encase his coffin when buried in his native country of France.

The telegraph's first transmission from the Capitol building in Washington, D.C to Baltimore by Samuel Morse
"What hath God wrought" Number 23:23

Regarded as one of America's greatest leaders, many American artists celebrated Abraham Lincoln while he was alive and in the years following his death with numerous portraits.

Lincoln also has a connection to the postal world. In 1833 he assumed the duties of the postmaster of New Salem, Illinois, becoming the only man to serve as a postmaster and later president. Given his importance to this country and his relationship with the post, Lincoln has been featured on many postage stamps. For example, in 1959, the government released a commemorative series celebrating the 150th anniversary of the president's birth.

https://postalmuseum.si.edu/exhibition/american-art-on-postage-stamps-american-leaders/remembering-abraham-lincoln

The earliest usage of this phrase can be found in the introduction to an English translation of the Bible by John Wycliffe in 1384 "This Bible is for the Government of the People, by the People, and for the People."

By the President of the United States of America. A Proclamation.

Whereas, the Senate of the United States, devoutly recognizing the Supreme Authority and just Government of Almighty God, in all the affairs of men and of nations, has, by a resolution, requested the President to designate and set apart a day for National prayer and humiliation.

And whereas it is the duty of nations as well as of men, to own their dependence upon the overruling power of God, to confess their sins and transgressions, in humble sorrow, yet with assured hope that genuine repentance will lead to mercy and pardon; and to recognize the sublime truth, announced in the Holy Scriptures and proven by all history, that those nations only are blessed whose God is the Lord.

And, insomuch as we know that, by His divine law, nations like individuals are subjected to punishments and chastisements in this world, may we not justly fear that the awful calamity of civil war, which now desolates the land, may be but a punishment, inflicted upon us, for our presumptuous sins, to the needful end of our national reformation as a whole People? We have been the recipients of the choicest bounties of Heaven. We have been preserved, these many years, in peace and prosperity. We have grown in numbers, wealth and power, as no other nation has ever grown. *But we have forgotten God. We have forgotten the gracious hand which preserved us in peace, and multiplied and enriched and strengthened us; and we have vainly imagined, in the deceitfulness of our hearts, that all these blessings were produced by some superior wisdom and virtue of our own. Intoxicated with unbroken success, we have become too self-sufficient to feel the necessity of redeeming and preserving grace, too proud to pray to the God that made us!*

It behooves us then, to humble ourselves before the offended Power, to confess our national sins, and to pray for clemency and forgiveness.

Now, therefore, in compliance with the request, and fully concurring in the views of the Senate, I do, by this my proclamation, designate and set apart Thursday, the 30th. day of April, 1863, as a day of national humiliation, fasting and prayer. And I do hereby request all the People to abstain, on that day, from their ordinary secular pursuits, and to unite, at their several places of public worship and their respective homes, in keeping the day holy to the Lord, and devoted to the humble discharge of the religious duties proper to that solemn occasion.

All this being done, in sincerity and truth, let us then rest humbly in the hope authorized by the Divine teachings, that the united cry of the Nation will be heard on high, and answered with blessings, no less than the pardon of our national sins, and the restoration of our now divided and suffering Country, to its former happy condition of unity and peace.

In witness whereof, I have hereunto set my hand and caused the seal of the United States to be affixed.

Done at the City of Washington, this thirtieth day of March, in the year of our Lord one thousand eight hundred and sixty-three, and of the Independence of the United States the eighty seventh.

By the President: Abraham Lincoln
William H. Seward, Secretary of State.

Abraham Lincoln appeared for the first time on a U.S. postage stamp with the issue of 1866, released on April 14, 1866, the first anniversary of his death. Up until this time only the portrayals of Washington, Franklin, Jefferson and Jackson were found on U.S. postage.

November 19, 1863 Gettysburg Cemetery

Four score and seven years ago our fathers brought forth, upon this continent, a new nation, conceived in Liberty, and dedicated to the proposition that all men are created equal.

Now we are engaged in a great civil war, testing whether that nation, or any nation so conceived, and so dedicated, can long endure. We are met on a great battle-field of that war. We have come to dedicate a portion of that field, as a final resting-place for those who here gave their lives, that that nation might live. It is altogether fitting and proper that we should do this.

But, in a larger sense, we can not dedicate, we can not consecrate we can not hallow this ground. The brave men, living and dead, who struggled here, have consecrated it far above our poor power to add or detract. The world will little note, nor long remember what we say here, but it can never forget what they did here.

It is for us, the living, rather, to be dedicated here to the unfinished work which they who fought here, have, thus far, so nobly advanced. It is rather for us to be here dedicated to the great task remaining before us that from these honored dead we take increased devotion to that cause for which they here gave the last full measure of devotion that we here highly resolve that these dead shall not have died in vain that this nation, under God, shall have a new birth of freedom and that government of the people, by the people, for the people, shall not perish from the earth.

Lincoln's 2nd Inaugural Address

(Lincoln's Sermon on the Mount)

SATURDAY, MARCH 4, 1865

Fellow-Countrymen, at this second appearing to take the oath of the Presidential office there is less occasion for an extended address than there was at the first. Then a statement somewhat in detail of a course to be pursued seemed fitting and proper. Now, at the expiration of four years, during which public declarations have been constantly called forth on every point and phase of the great contest which still absorbs the attention and engrosses the energies of the nation, little that is new could be presented. The progress of our arms, upon which all else chiefly depends, is as well known to the public as to myself, and it is, I trust, reasonably satisfactory and encouraging to all. With high hope for the future, no prediction in regard to it is ventured.

On the occasion corresponding to this four years ago all thoughts were anxiously directed to an impending civil war. All dreaded it, all sought to avert it. While the inaugural address was being delivered from this place, devoted
altogether to saving the Union without war, insurgent agents were in the city

seeking to destroy it without war--
seeking to dissolve the Union and
divide effects by negotiation. Both
parties deprecated war, but one of them
would make war rather than let the
nation survive, and the other would
accept war rather than let it perish, and
the war came.

One-eighth of the whole population
were colored slaves, not distributed
generally over the Union, but localized
in the southern part of it. These slaves
constituted a peculiar and powerful
interest. All knew that this interest was
somehow the cause of the war. To
strengthen, perpetuate, and extend this

interest was the object for which the insurgents would rend the Union even by war, while the Government claimed no right to do more than to restrict the territorial enlargement of it. Neither party expected for the war the magnitude or the duration which it has already attained. Neither anticipated that the cause of the conflict might cease with or even before the conflict itself should cease. Each looked for an easier triumph,

and a result less fundamental and astounding. Both read the same Bible and pray to the same God, and each invokes His aid against the other. It may seem strange that any men should dare to ask a just God's assistance in wringing their bread from the sweat of other men's faces; but let us judge not, that we be not judged. The prayers of both could not be answered. That of neither has been answered fully. The Almighty has His own purposes. "Woe unto the world because of offenses; for it must needs be that offenses come, but woe to that man by whom the offense cometh." If we shall suppose that American slavery is one of those offenses which, in the providence of God, must needs come, but which, having continued through His appointed time, He now wills to remove, and that He gives to both North and South this terrible war as the woe due to those by whom the offense came, shall we discern therein any departure from those divine attributes which the believers in a living God always ascribe to Him? Fondly do we hope, fervently do we pray, that this mighty scourge of war may speedily pass away. Yet, if God wills that it continue until all the wealth piled by the bondsman's two hundred and fifty years of unrequited toil shall be sunk, and until every drop of blood drawn with the lash shall be paid by another drawn with the sword, as was said three thousand years ago, so still it must be said "the judgments of the Lord are true and righteous altogether."

"With malice toward none, with charity for all, with firmness in the right as God gives us to see the right, let us strive on to finish the work we are in, to bind up the nation's wounds, to care for him who shall have borne the battle and for his widow and his orphan, to do all which may achieve

History is not history unless it is the truth.

Abraham Lincoln

and cherish a just and lasting peace
among ourselves and with all
nations."

Originally published as Chronological Chart of Ancient, Modern and Biblical History by Presbyterian missionary Sebastian C. Adams -The Walchart is a synchronological timeline that graphically depicts the history of mankind from 4004 BC, the beginning of man, to modern times, based on the Bible and merging with history on the elaborately detailed pages following.

The original version was published in 1871 and was printed by the authority of the United States Congress. Over the next few pages note the Biblical events highlighted in this remarkable endeavor meriting the stamp of approval from Congress.

From Adams Map of History
"In the beginning God created the Heavens and the the Earth." - Gen. 1-1

On November 24, 1859 Charles Darwin's Origin of Species was published, receiving instant acclaim in the academic world. However 11 years later, this chart is entered according to an act of Congress in the year A.D (Anno Dominea) 1871 by S.C Adams in the office of the Librarian of Congress at Washington, D.C. Clearly showing a Biblical Worldview beginning with the Genesis account of Creation. "In the beginning God Created the Heaven and the Earth." Gen. 1:1 and the narrative clearly showing a Divine Creator creating Adam and Eve.

The narrative continues with the story of Cain and Able, Able proving an acceptable sacrifice and Cain in jealously killing his brother Able.

From Adams Map of History
Entered According to Act of Congress in
the year A.D. 1871 by S.C Adams in the
office of the Librarian of Congress at
Washington, D.C.

THE WHITE HOUSE
WASHINGTON

January 25, 1941

To the Armed Forces:

As Commander-in-Chief I take
pleasure in commending the reading
of the Bible to all who serve in the
armed forces of the United States.
Throughout the centuries men of many
faiths and diverse origins have
found in the Sacred Book words of
wisdom, counsel and inspiration.
It is a fountain of strength and
now, as always, an aid in attaining
the highest aspirations of the
human soul.

Very sincerely yours,

Franklin D. Roosevelt

Franklin D. Roosevelt.

The New Testament with letter of encouragement
by President Franklin Roosevelt commending the
reading of the Bible. Inserted is the facing page of
this endorsement with the Christian flag flown
above the American Flag as is acceptable for
divines services.

80

83

On November 1, 1965, the subject for its 4th Christmas stamp, was of the Christmas angel Gabriel.

It stirred up some controversy among those who felt it was a constitutional issue mixing church and state. Melvin Laird, a Wisconsin representative in 1965, complained that the post office should have a religious Christmas stamp. He contended that nobody would consider that a violation of the separation of church and state since the holiday was such a part of American culture

Others argued that people weren't really wanting or requesting a religious themed stamp because nearly a billion non-religious Christmas stamps were sold the year before – so why create one now.

Postmaster General John A. Gronouski, ended up consulting with government lawyers and what resulted was the publication of green and yellow stamp of a watercolor by Lucille Gloria Chabot of an 1840 weather vane entitled "Gabriel Weather Vane." The original painting is part of the collection at the National Gallery of Art in Washington, D.C. It seemed to solve the issue by providing a religious themed stamp for those who wanted one while detractors could see it also as a simple depiction of classic American Folk Art.

The Citizens' Stamp Advisory Committee (CSAC) reviews suggestions for new stamp designs and recommends these designs to the postmaster general. Following years of customer requests, CSAC recommended that the U.S. Post Office Department issue a Christmas stamp. The first Christmas stamp — Holiday Celebrations: Wreath and Candles — was issued in 1962.

Three years later, CSAC faced the question "How could you issue a stamp to commemorate Christmas without addressing the central theme of religion?"

Their answer was a stamp issued with an image of a church weather vane in the shape of the angel Gabriel blowing a trumpet — a stamp that might be considered religious.

This did not end the controversy because stamp collectors, as well as the general public, was looking for a Christmas stamp with a religious image. CSAC found the answer — stamp images based on paintings of the Madonna and Child would not violate [their perception of] the Establishment Clause of the First Amendment to the Constitution.

13 Folds in the Ceremonial Flag

The **first** fold of our flag is a symbol of life.
The **second** fold is a symbol of our belief in eternal life.
The **third** fold is made in honor and remembrance of the veteran departing our ranks, and who gave a portion of his or her life for the defense of our country to attain peace throughout the world.
The **fourth** fold represents our weaker nature; as American citizens trusting in God, it is to Him we turn in times of

peace, as well as in times of war, for His divine guidance.

The **fifth** fold is a tribute to our country, for in the words of Stephen Decatur, "Our country, in dealing with other countries, may she always be right, but it is still our country, right or wrong."

The **sixth** fold is for where our hearts lie. It is with our heart that we pledge allegiance to the flag of the United States of America, and to the republic for which it stands, one nation under God, indivisible, with liberty and justice for all.

The **seventh** fold is a tribute to our armed forces, for it is through the armed forces that we protect our country and our flag against all enemies, whether they be found within or without the boundaries of our republic.

The **eighth** fold is a tribute to the one who entered into the valley of the shadow of death, that we might see the light of day, and to honor our mother, for whom it flies on Mother's Day.

The **ninth** fold is a tribute to womanhood, for it has been through their faith, love, loyalty and devotion that the character of the men and women who have made this country great have been molded.

The **10th** fold is a tribute to father, for he, too, has given his sons and daughters for the defense of our country since he or she was first born.

The **11th** fold, in the eyes of Hebrew citizens, represents the lower portion of the seal of King David and King Solomon and glorifies, in their eyes, the God of Abraham, Isaac and Jacob.

The **12th** fold, in the eyes of a Christian citizen, represents an emblem of eternity and glorifies, in their eyes, God the Father, the Son and Holy Ghost.

When the flag is completely folded, the stars are uppermost, reminding us of our national motto, "In God We Trust."

After the flag is completely folded and tucked in, it has the appearance of a cocked hat, ever reminding us of the soldiers who served under Gen. George Washington and the sailors and Marines who served under Capt. John Paul Jones and were followed by their comrades and shipmates in the U.S. Armed Forces, preserving for us the rights, privileges and freedoms we enjoy today.

The source and the date of origin of this Flag Folding Procedure is unknown, however some sources attribute it to the Gold Star Mothers of America while others to an Air Force chaplain stationed at the United States Air Force Academy. Others consider it to be an urban legend. It is provided as a patriotic service to all.

92

During the Cold War, President Eisenhower attended Sunday services at New York Avenue Presbyterian Church in Washington, DC. The topic of the message was adding the word "under God" to our pledge of Allegiance. He was impressed enough to give his support to the idea. During his Presidency the first In God we trust stamp was minted and has since been reissued as a statement to clearly distinguish us from the menace of godless atheism found in the Soviet Union and Communist Countries.

Mark 8:34 Jesus said: "Whosoever will come after me, let him deny himself, take up his cross and follow me."

The bold blue "Follow Me" patch, the well known symbol of Fort Benning, U.S. Army Infantry Center and Schools...proudly undertake the responsibility of representing not only the great Soldiers that comprise Fort Benning, but also in representing those who serve and sacrifice everyday, past, present and future in our great Army. AIRBORNE! www.benning.army.mil

Leaders don't send their soldiers in to harms way, they lead them with "Follow Me".

Earthrise photograph by William Anders from Apollo 8 December 24, 1968

William Anders
"We are now approaching lunar sunrise, and for all the people back on Earth, the crew of Apollo 8 has a

message that we would like to send to you."

In the beginning God created the heaven and the earth.

And the earth was without form, and void; and darkness was upon the face of the deep.

And the Spirit of God moved upon the face of the waters. And God said, Let there be light: and there was light.

And God saw the light, that it was good: and God divided the light from the darkness.[4]

James Lovell

And God called the light Day, and the darkness he called Night. And the evening and the morning were the first day.

And God said, Let there be a firmament in the midst of the waters, and let it divide the waters from the waters.

And God made the firmament, and divided the waters which were under the firmament from the waters which

were above the firmament: and it was so.
And God called the firmament Heaven. And the evening and the morning were the second day."[4]

Frank Borman

And God said, Let the waters under the heaven be gathered together unto one place, and let the dry land appear: and it was so.

And God called the dry land Earth; and the gathering together of the waters called he Seas: and God saw that it was good."

"And from the crew of Apollo 8, we close with good night, good luck, a Merry Christmas – and God bless all of you, all of you on the good Earth.

Buzz Aldrin from his book
Magnificent Desolation

Landing on the moon is not quite the same thing as arriving at Grandmother's for Thanksgiving. You don't hop out of the lunar module the moment the engine stops and yell, "We're here! We're here!" Getting out of the LM takes a lot of preparation, so we had built in several extra hours to our flight plan. We also figured it was wise to allow more time rather than less for our initial activities after landing, just in case anything had gone wrong during the flight.

According to our schedule, we were supposed to eat a meal, rest awhile, and then sleep for seven hours after arriving on the moon. After all, we had already worked a long, full day and we wanted to be fresh for our extra-vehicular activity (EVA). Mission

Control had notified the media that they could take a break and catch their breath since there wouldn't be much happening for several hours as we rested. But it was hard to rest with all that adrenaline pumping through our systems.

Nevertheless, in an effort to remain calm and collected, I decided that this would be an excellent time for a ceremony I had planned as an expression of gratitude and hope. Weeks before, as the Apollo mission drew near, I had originally asked Dean Woodruff, pastor at Webster Presbyterian Church, where my family and

I attended services when I was home in Houston, to help me come up with something I could do on the moon, some appropriate symbolic act regarding the universality of seeking.
I wanted to do something positive for the world, so the spiritual aspect

appealed greatly to me, I had thought in terms of doing something overtly patriotic, but everything we came up with sounded trite and jingoistic. I settled on a well-known expression of spirituality: celebrating the first Christian Communion on the moon, much as Christopher Columbus and other explorers had done when they first landed in their "new world."

In the Beginning God
Genesis 1:1

The first four words of the Bible.
If you can believe those words,
everything else is easy.

Fred W. Haise
March 17, 2016

The attached "Microfiche Bible" was carried around the moon on the April 11-17, 1970 flight of Apollo 13. At just under 56 hours into the mission, an oxygen tank explosion resulted in a major loss of electrical power to the Command and Service Module. This event caused a scrub of the lunar landing and forced us to move into the Lunar Module in order to survive a four day journey around the moon and return back to earth. The Mission stands out an epic example of training and teamwork overcoming a great challenge. Many individuals from NASA and our contractor team worked around the clock to ensure our safe return. This drama was captured in the Hollywood Movie *Apollo 13*.

This "Microfiche Bible" has been in my personal space artifact collection since 1970.

Sincerely,

Fred W. Haise
Apollo 13 Lunar Module Pilot

A Microfilm Bible that flew on Apollo 13 in 1970 is being auctioned off with bidding starting at $50,000.

The "Lunar Bibles" were created by the Apollo Prayer League, whose overreaching mission was to pray for the safety of the astronauts and the skill of NASA employees who built the rockets and, land a Bible on the moon. The Microfilm Bible flew onboard the Apollo 13 mission to the moon and comes from the personal collection of former NASA astronaut Fred Haise, who flew as lunar module pilot on Apollo 13. Apollo 13 never made it to the moon. Two days into the flight, an explosion on the service module forced the three astronauts to use the lunar module as a lifeboat. NASA aborted the moon landing and focused instead on finding a way to get the crew back to Earth safely.

Newsmax 12/12/17

On a recent tour of the Holy Land, our guide was exceptional, adding many stories and insights making the trip especially enjoyable. When we were at the South end of the Temple Mount, our guide told of when Neil Armstrong took a tour of the Holy Land he kept pestering his guide with "Did Jesus walk here?" Finally, as they stood on the South End of the Temple Mount the guide said "we know Jesus would have walked on these stones". Neil Armstrong ran up and down the stones like a school boy then said "It means more to me to walk on these stones than the Moon."

They shall hunger no more neither
thirst anymore Revelation 7:16
At the Valley Forge Memorial.
(photo Wikipedia)

Incorporating the heartfelt patriotism
voiced in our National Anthem
reflected in a 1945 Recruiting Poster

Preambles in our State Constitutions *

Alabama

Preamble:

We, the people of the State of Alabama, in order to establish justice, insure domestic tranquillity, and secure the blessings of liberty to ourselves and our posterity, invoking the favor and guidance of **Almighty God**, do ordain and establish the following Constitution and form of government for the State of Alabama:

Section 1:

That all men are equally free and independent; that they are endowed by their **Creator** with certain inalienable rights; that among these are life, liberty and the pursuit of happiness.

Section 186, witness oath:

"... so help me **God**."

Section 279, oath of office:

"So help me **God**."

Alaska

Preamble:

We the people of Alaska, grateful to **God** and to those who founded our nation and pioneered this great land, in order to secure and transmit to succeeding generations our heritage of political, civil, and religious liberty within the Union of States, do ordain and establish this constitution for the State of Alaska.

Arizona

Preamble:

We, the people of the State of Arizona, grateful to **Almighty God** for our liberties, do ordain this Constitution.

Arkansas

Preamble:

We, the People of the State of Arkansas, grateful to **Almighty God** for the privilege of choosing our own form of government; for our civil and religious liberty; and desiring to perpetuate its blessings, and secure the same to our selves and posterity; do ordain and establish this Constitution.

Article 2, Section 24:

All men have a natural and indefeasible right to worship **Almighty God** according to the dictates of their own consciences;

Article 19:

No person who denies the being of a **God** shall hold any office in the civil departments of this State, nor be competent to testify as a witness in any Court.

Terminus:

... in the year of our **Lord** one thousand eight hundred and seventy four ...

California

Preamble:

We, the People of the State of California, grateful to **Almighty God** for our freedom, in order to secure and perpetuate its blessings, do establish this Constitution.

Colorado

We, the people of Colorado, with profound reverence for the **Supreme Ruler of the Universe**, in order to form a more independent and perfect government; establish justice; insure tranquillity; provide for the common defense; promote the general welfare and secure the blessings of liberty to ourselves and our posterity, do ordain and establish this constitution for the "State of Colorado".

Article 5, Section 45:

... in the year of our **Lord** 1885 ...

Terminus:

... in the year of our **Lord** one thousand eight hundred and seventy-six ...

Connecticut

Preamble:

The People of Connecticut acknowledging with gratitude, the good providence of **God**, in having permitted them to enjoy a free government; do, in order more effectually to define, secure, and perpetuate the liberties, rights and privileges which they have derived from their ancestors;

hereby, after a careful consideration and revision, ordain and establish the following constitution and form of civil government.

Article 11, Section 1, oath of office:

... So help you **God**.

Delaware

Preamble:

Through **Divine goodness**, all men have by nature the rights of worshiping and serving their **Creator** according to the dictates of their consciences, of enjoying and defending life and liberty, of acquiring and protecting reputation and property, and in general of obtaining objects suitable to their condition, without injury by one to another; and as these rights are essential to their welfare, for due exercise thereof, power is inherent in them; and therefore all just authority in the institutions of political society is derived from the people, and established with their consent, to advance their happiness; and they may for this end, as circumstances require, from time to time, alter their Constitution of government.

Article 1, Section 1:

Although it is the duty of all men frequently to assemble together for the public worship of **Almighty God**; and piety and morality, on which the prosperity of communities depends, are hereby promoted; yet no man shall or ought to be compelled to attend any religious worship, to contribute to the erection or support of any place of worship, or to the maintenance of any ministry, against his own free will and consent;

Article 5, Section 2:

... in the year of our **Lord**, Nineteen Hundred ...

Article 14, Section 1, oath of office:

"... so help me **God**."

Terminus:

... in the year of our **Lord** One Thousand Eight Hundred and Ninety-Seven ...

Florida

Preamble:

We, the people of the State of Florida, being grateful to **Almighty God** for our constitutional liberty, in order to secure its benefits, perfect our government, insure domestic tranquility, maintain public order, and guarantee equal civil and political rights to all, do ordain and establish this constitution.

Article 2, Section 5, oath of office:

"So help me **God**."

Georgia

Preamble:

To perpetuate the principles of free government, insure justice to all, preserve peace, promote the interest and happiness of the citizen and of the family, and transmit to posterity the enjoyment of liberty, we the people of Georgia, relying upon the protection and guidance of **Almighty God**, do ordain and establish this Constitution.

Hawaii

Preamble:

We, the people of Hawaii, grateful for **Divine Guidance**, and mindful of our Hawaiian heritage and uniqueness as an island State, dedicate our efforts to fulfill the philosophy decreed by the Hawaii State motto, "Ua mau ke ea o ka aina i ka pono."

Article 7, Section 13:

Bonds issued by or on behalf of the State or by any political subdivision to meet appropriations for any fiscal period in anticipation of the collection of revenues for such period or to meet casual deficits or failures of revenue, if required to be paid within one year, and bonds issued by or on behalf of the State to suppress insurrection, to repel invasion, to defend the State in war or to meet emergencies caused by disaster or act of **God**.

Idaho

Preamble:

We, the people of the State of Idaho, grateful to **Almighty God** for our freedom, to secure its blessings and promote our common welfare do establish this Constitution.

Illinois

<u>Preamble:</u>

We, the People of the State of Illinois — grateful to **Almighty God** for the civil, political and religious liberty which **He** has permitted us to enjoy and seeking **His** blessing upon our endeavors — in order to provide for the health, safety and welfare of the people; maintain a representative and orderly government; eliminate poverty and inequality; assure legal, social and economic justice; provide opportunity for the fullest development of the individual; insure domestic tranquility; provide for the common defense; and secure the blessings of freedom and liberty to ourselves and our posterity — do ordain and establish this Constitution for the State of Illinois.

Indiana

<u>Preamble:</u>

TO THE END, that justice be established, public order maintained, and liberty perpetuated; WE, the People of the State of Indiana, grateful to **ALMIGHTY GOD** for the free exercise of the right to choose our own form of government, do ordain this Constitution.

Article 1, Section 1:

WE DECLARE, That all people are created equal; that they are endowed by their **CREATOR** with certain inalienable rights;

Article 1, Section 2:

All people shall be secured in the natural right to worship **ALMIGHTY GOD**, according to the dictates of their own consciences.

Iowa

Preamble:

WE THE PEOPLE OF THE STATE OF IOWA, grateful to the **Supreme Being** for the blessings hitherto enjoyed, and feeling our dependence on **Him** for a continuation of those blessings, do ordain and establish a free and independent government, by the name of the State of Iowa, the boundaries whereof shall be as follows:

Article 9, Part 2, Section 3:t 2, Section 3:

... in the year of our **Lord** one thousand eight hundred and forty-one ...

Kansas

Preamble:

We, the people of Kansas, grateful to **Almighty God** for our civil and religious privileges, in order to insure the full enjoyment of our rights as American citizens, do ordain and establish this constitution of the state of Kansas, with the following boundaries, to wit:

Bill of Rights, Section 7:

The right to worship **God** according to the dictates of conscience shall never be infringed;

Kentucky

Preamble:

We, the people of the Commonwealth of Kentucky, grateful to **Almighty God** for the civil, political and religious liberties we enjoy, and invoking the continuance of these blessings, do ordain and establish this Constitution.

Section 1, Clause 2:

The right of worshipping **Almighty God** according to the dictates of their consciences.

Section 228, oath of office:

... so help me **God**.

Section 232:

The manner of administering an oath or affirmation shall be such as is most consistent with the conscience of the deponent, and shall be esteemed by the General Assembly the most solemn appeal to **God**.

Terminus:

... in the year of our **Lord** one thousand eight hundred and ninety-one ...

Louisiana

<u>Preamble:</u>

We, the people of Louisiana, grateful to **Almighty God** for the civil, political, economic, and religious liberties we enjoy, and desiring to protect individual rights to life, liberty, and property; afford opportunity for the fullest development of the individual; assure equality of rights; promote the health, safety, education, and welfare of the people; maintain a representative and orderly government; ensure domestic tranquility; provide for the common defense; and secure the blessings of freedom and justice to ourselves and our posterity, do ordain and establish this constitution.

<u>Article 10, Section 30, oath of office:</u>

"... so help me **God**."

Maine

<u>Preamble:</u>

We the people of Maine, in order to establish justice, insure tranquility, provide for our mutual defense, promote our common welfare, and secure to ourselves and our posterity the blessings of liberty, acknowledging with grateful hearts the goodness of the **Sovereign Ruler of the Universe** in affording us an opportunity, so favorable to the design; and, imploring **God**'s aid and direction in its accomplishment, do agree to form ourselves into a free and independent State, by the style and title of the State of Maine and do ordain and establish the following Constitution for the government of the same.

Article 1, Section 3:

All individuals have a natural and unalienable right to worship **Almighty God** according to the dictates of their own consciences, and no person shall be hurt, molested or restrained in that person's liberty or estate for worshipping **God** in the manner and season most agreeable to the dictates of that person's own conscience, nor for that person's religious professions or sentiments, provided that that person does not disturb the public peace, nor obstruct others in their religious worship;

Article 9, Section 1, oath of office

"So help me **God**."

Article 9, Section 1, alternative oath of office

"So help me **God**."

Maryland

Preamble:

We, the People of the State of Maryland, grateful to **Almighty God** for our civil and religious liberty, and taking into our serious consideration the best means of establishing a good Constitution in this State for the sure foundation and more permanent security thereof, declare:

Declaration of Rights, Article 36:

That as it is the duty of every man to worship **God** in such manner as he thinks most acceptable to **Him**, all persons are equally entitled to protection in their religious liberty; ... nor shall any person, otherwise competent, be deemed incompetent as a witness, or juror, on account of his religious belief; provided, he believes in the existence of **God**, and that under **His** dispensation such person will be held morally accountable for his acts, and be rewarded or punished therefor either in this world or in the world to come.

Nothing shall prohibit or require the making reference to belief in, reliance upon, or invoking the aid of **God** or a **Supreme Being** in any governmental or public document, proceeding, activity, ceremony, school, institution, or place.

Declaration of Rights, Article 37:

That no religious test ought ever to be required as a qualification for any office of profit or trust in this State, other than a declaration of belief in the existence of **God**; nor shall the Legislature prescribe any other oath of office than the oath prescribed by this Constitution.

Declaration of Rights, Article 39:

That the manner of administering an oath or affirmation to any person, ought to be such as those of the religious persuasion, profession, or denomination, of which he is a member, generally esteem the most effectual confirmation by the attestation of the **Divine Being**.

Massachusetts

Preamble:

We, therefore, the people of Massachusetts, acknowledging, with grateful hearts, the goodness of the great **Legislator of the universe**, in affording us, in the course of **His** providence, an opportunity, deliberately and peaceably, without fraud, violence or surprise, of entering into an original, explicit, and solemn compact with each other; and of forming a new constitution of civil government, for ourselves and posterity; and devoutly imploring **His** direction in so interesting a design, do agree upon, ordain and establish the following Declaration of Rights, and Frame of Government, as the Constitution of the Commonwealth of Massachusetts.

Part 1, Article 2:

It is the right as well as the duty of all men in society, publicly, and at stated seasons to worship the **Supreme Being**, the great **Creator and Preserver of the universe**. And no subject shall be hurt, molested, or restrained, in his person, liberty, or estate, for worshipping **God** in the manner and season most agreeable to the dictates of his own conscience;

Chapter 5, Section 1, Article 1:

Whereas our wise and pious ancestors, so early as the year one thousand six hundred and thirty-six, laid the foundation of Harvard College, in which university many persons of great eminence have, by the blessing of **God**, been initiated in those arts and sciences, which qualified them for public employments, both in church and state: and whereas the encouragement of arts and sciences, and all good literature, tends to the honor of **God**, the advantage of the Christian religion, and the great benefit of this and the other United States of America ...

Chapter 6, Article 1:

"So help me, **God**."

Chapter 6, Article 10:

... in the year of our **Lord** one thousand seven hundred and ninety-five ...

Chapter 6, Article 12:

... in the year of our **Lord** one thousand eight hundred and thirty-seven ...

... in the year of our **Lord** one thousand eight hundred and thirty-seven ...

Amendments, Article 6, oath of office:

"So help me **God**."

Amendments, Article 11:

As the public worship of **God** and instructions in piety, religion and morality, promote the happiness and prosperity of a people and the security of a republican government;

Michigan

Preamble:

We, the people of the State of Michigan, grateful to **Almighty God** for the blessings of freedom, and earnestly desiring to secure these blessings undiminished to ourselves and our posterity, do ordain and establish this constitution.

Article 1, Section 4: Every person shall be at liberty to worship **God** according to the dictates of his own conscience.

Minnesota

Preamble:

We, the people of the state of Minnesota, grateful to **God** for our civil and religious liberty, and desiring to perpetuate its blessings and secure the same to ourselves and our posterity, do ordain and establish this Constitution.

Article 1, Section 16:

The right of every man to worship **God** according to the dictates of his own conscience shall never be infringed;

Mississippi

Preamble:

We, the people of Mississippi in convention assembled, grateful to **Almighty God**, and invoking **his** blessing on our work, do ordain and establish this constitution.

Article 4, Section 40, oath of office:

"So help me **God**."

Article 6, Section 155, oath of office:

"So help me **God**."

Article 14, Section 268, oath of office:

"So help me **God**."

Missouri

Preamble:

We the people of Missouri, with profound reverence for the **Supreme Ruler of the Universe**, and grateful for **His** goodness, do establish this constitution for the better government of the state.

Article 1, Section 5:

That all men have a natural and indefeasible right to worship **Almighty God** according to the dictates of their own consciences;

Montana

Preamble:

We the people of Montana grateful to **God** for the quiet beauty of our state, the grandeur of our mountains, the vastness of our rolling plains, and desiring to improve the quality of life, equality of opportunity and to secure the blessings of liberty for this and future generations do ordain and establish this constitution.

Article 3, Section 3, oath of office:

"... (so help me **God**)."

Nebraska

Preamble:

We, the people, grateful to **Almighty God** for our freedom, do ordain and establish the following declaration of rights and frame of government, as the Constitution of the State of Nebraska.

Article 1, Section 4:

All persons have a natural and indefeasible right to worship **Almighty God** according to the dictates of their own consciences.

Nevada

Preamble:

We the people of the State of Nevada Grateful to **Almighty God** for our freedom in order to secure its blessings, insure domestic tranquility, and form a more perfect Government, do establish this Constitution.

Article 15, Section 2, oath of office:

... so help me **God**.

Terminus:

... in the year of our **Lord** One Thousand Eight Hundred and Sixty Four ...

New Hampshire

Part 1, Article 5:

Every individual has a natural and unalienable right to worship **God** according to the dictates of his own conscience, and reason; and no subject shall be hurt, molested, or restrained, in his person, liberty, or estate, for worshipping **God** in the manner and season most agreeable to the dictates of his own conscience;

Part 2, Article 84, oath of office:

So help me **God**.

New Jersey

Preface:

... in the year of our **Lord** one thousand nine hundred and forty-seven.

Preamble:

We, the people of the State of New Jersey, grateful to **Almighty God** for the civil and religious liberty which **He** hath so long permitted us to enjoy, and looking to **Him** for a blessing upon our endeavors to secure and transmit the same unimpaired to succeeding generations, do ordain and establish this Constitution.

Article 1, Section 3:

No person shall be deprived of the inestimable privilege of worshipping **Almighty God** in a manner agreeable to the dictates of his own conscience;

Article 8, Section 2:

Nor shall anything in this paragraph contained apply to the creation of any debts or liabilities for purposes of war, or to repel invasion, or to suppress insurrection or to meet an emergency caused by disaster or act of **God**.

Article 10, Clause 5:

... in the year of our **Lord** one thousand nine hundred and forty-eight.

New Mexico

Preamble:

We, the people of New Mexico, grateful to **Almighty God** for the blessings of liberty, in order to secure the advantages of a state government, do ordain and establish this constitution.

Article 2, Section 11:

Every man shall be free to worship **God** according to the dictates of his own conscience, and no person shall ever be molested or denied any civil or political right or privilege on account of his religious opinion or mode of religious worship.

New York

Preamble:

We The People of the State of New York, grateful to **Almighty God** for our Freedom, in order to secure its blessings, DO ESTABLISH THIS CONSTITUTION.

North Carolina

Preamble:

We, the people of the State of North Carolina, grateful to **Almighty God**, the **Sovereign Ruler**

135

of Nations, for the preservation of the American Union and the existence of our civil, political and religious liberties, and acknowledging our dependence upon **Him** for the continuance of those blessings to us and our posterity, do, for the more certain security thereof and for the better government of this State, ordain and establish this Constitution.

Article 1, Section 1:

We hold it to be self-evident that all persons are created equal; that they are endowed by their **Creator** with certain inalienable rights; that among these are life, liberty, the enjoyment of the fruits of their own labor, and the pursuit of happiness.

Article 1, Section 13:

All persons have a natural and inalienable right to worship **Almighty God** according to the dictates of their own consciences, and no human authority shall, in any case whatever, control or interfere with the rights of conscience.

Article 6, Section 7, oath of office:

"... so help me **God**."

Article 6, Section 8:

The following persons shall be disqualified for office:

First, any person who shall deny the being of **Almighty God**.

North Dakota

Preamble:

We, the people of North Dakota, grateful to **Almighty God** for the blessings of civil and religious liberty, do ordain and establish this constitution.

Article 11, Section 4, oath of office:

"... so help me **God**."

Ohio

Preamble:

We, the people of the State of Ohio, grateful to **Almighty God** for our freedom, to secure its blessings and promote our common welfare, do establish this Constitution.

Article 1, Section 7:

All men have a natural and indefensible right to worship **Almighty God** according to the dictates of their own conscience.

Terminus:

... in the year of our **Lord**, one thousand eight hundred and fifty-one ...

Oklahoma

Preamble:

Invoking the guidance of **Almighty God**, in order to secure and perpetuate the blessing of liberty; to secure just and rightful government; to promote our mutual welfare and happiness, we, the people of the State of Oklahoma, do ordain and establish this Constitution.

Terminus:

... in the year of our **Lord** one thousand nine hundred and seven ...

Oregon

Article 1, Section 2:

All men shall be secure in the Natural right, to worship **Almighty God** according to the dictates of their own consciences.

Pennsylvania

Preamble:

WE, the people of the Commonwealth of Pennsylvania, grateful to **Almighty God** for the blessings of civil and religious liberty, and humbly invoking **His** guidance, do ordain and establish this Constitution.

Article 1, Section 3:

All men have a natural and indefeasible right to worship **Almighty God** according to the dictates of their own consciences;

Article 1, Section 4:

No person who acknowledges the being of a **God** and a future state of rewards and punishments shall, on account of his religious sentiments, be disqualified to hold any office or place of trust or profit under this Commonwealth.

Rhode Island

Preamble:

We, the people of the State of Rhode Island and Providence Plantations, grateful to **Almighty**

God for the civil and religious liberty which **He** hath so long permitted us to enjoy, and looking to **Him** for a blessing upon our endeavors to secure and to transmit the same, unimpaired, to succeeding generations, do ordain and establish this Constitution of government.

Article 1, Section 3:

Whereas **Almighty God** hath created the mind free; ... and that every person shall be free to worship **God** according to the dictates of such person's conscience, and to profess and by argument to maintain such person's opinion in matters of religion;

Article 3, Section 3, oath of office:

So help you **God**.

South Carolina

Preamble:

We, the people of the State of South Carolina, in Convention assembled, grateful to **God** for our liberties, do ordain and establish this Constitution for the preservation and perpetuation of the same.

Article 3, Section 26, oath of office:

"So help me **God**."

Article 6, Section 5, oath of office:

"So help me **God**."

Terminus:

... in the year of our **Lord**, one thousand Eight hundred and Ninety-five.

South Dakota

Preamble:

We, the people of South Dakota, grateful to **Almighty God** for our civil and religious liberties, in order to form a more perfect and independent government, establish justice, insure tranquillity, provide for the common defense, promote the general welfare and preserve to ourselves and to our posterity the blessings of liberty, do ordain and establish this Constitution for the state of South Dakota.

Article 3: The right to worship **God** according to the dictates of conscience shall never be infringed.

Article 21, Section 1:

Properly divided between the upper and lower edges of the circle shall appear the legend, "Under **God** the People Rule" which shall be the motto of the state of South Dakota.

Tennessee

Preamble:

... in the year of our **Lord** one thousand seven hundred and ninety-six ...

... in the year of our **Lord** one thousand eight hundred and thirty-three ...

... in the year of our **Lord** one thousand eight hundred and thirty-four ...

... in the year of our **Lord** one thousand eight hundred and thirty-five ...

... in the year of our **Lord** one thousand eight hundred and sixty-nine ...

... in the year of our **Lord** one thousand eight hundred and seventy ...

Article 1, Section 2:

That all men have a natural and indefeasible right to worship **Almighty God** according to the dictates of their own conscience;

Article 9, Section 1:

Whereas ministers of the Gospel are by their profession, dedicated to **God** and the care of souls, and ought not to be diverted from the great duties of their functions; therefore, no minister of the Gospel, or priest of any denomination whatever, shall be eligible to a seat in either House of the Legislature.

Article 9, Section 2:

No person who denies the being of **God**, or a future state of rewards and punishments, shall hold any office in the civil department of this state.

Texas

Preamble:

Humbly invoking the blessings of **Almighty God**, the people of the State of Texas, do ordain and establish this Constitution.

Article 1, Section 6:

All men have a natural and indefeasible right to worship **Almighty God** according to the dictates of their own consciences.

Article 16, Section 1, oath of office:

"... so help me **God**."

Utah

Preamble:

Grateful to **Almighty God** for life and liberty, we, the people of Utah, in order to secure and perpetuate the principles of free government, do ordain and establish this CONSTITUTION.

Terminus:

... in the year of our **Lord** one thousand eight hundred and ninety-five ...

Vermont

Chapter 1, Article 3:

That all persons have a natural and unalienable right, to worship **Almighty God**, according to the dictates of their own consciences and understandings, as in their opinion shall be regulated by the word of **God**; ... Nevertheless, every sect or denomination of Christians ought to observe the sabbath or **Lord**'s day, and keep up some sort of religious worship, which to them shall seem most agreeable to the revealed will of **God**.

Article 2, Section 16, oath of office:

So help you **God**.

Article 2, Section 17, oath of office:

So help you **God**.

Article 2, Section 56, oath of office:

So help you **God**.

Virginia

Article 1, Section 17:

That religion or the duty which we owe to our **Creator**, and the manner of discharging it, can be directed only by reason and conviction, not by force or violence;

Article 2, Section 7, oath of office:

"... (so help me **God**)."

Washington

Preamble:

We, the people of the State of Washington, grateful to the **Supreme Ruler of the Universe** for our liberties, do ordain this constitution.

West Virginia

Preamble:

Since through **Divine Providence** we enjoy the blessings of civil, political and religious liberty, we, the people of West Virginia, in and through the provisions of this Constitution, reaffirm our faith in and constant reliance upon **God** and seek diligently to promote, preserve and perpetuate good government in the state of West Virginia for the common welfare, freedom and security of ourselves and our posterity.

Wisconsin

Preamble:

We, the people of Wisconsin, grateful to **Almighty God** for our freedom, in order to secure its blessings, form a more perfect government, insure domestic tranquility and promote the general welfare, do establish this constitution.

Article 1, Section 18:

The right of every person to worship **Almighty God** according to the dictates of conscience shall never be infringed;

Wyoming

Preamble:

We, the people of the State of Wyoming, grateful to **God** for our civil, political and religious liberties, and desiring to secure them to ourselves and perpetuate them to our posterity, do ordain and establish this Constitution.

Terminus:

... in the year of our **Lord** one thousand eight hundred and eighty-nine.

American Samoa

<u>Article 5, Section 6, oath of office:</u>

So help me **God**.

Guam - Organic Act

<u>Subchapter 3, Section 1423d, oath of office:</u>

I solemnly swear (or affirm) in the presence of **Almighty God** that I will well and faithfully support the Constitution of the United States...

<u>Terminus:</u>

... in the year of our **Lord** nineteen hundred seventy-five ...

Puerto Rico

<u>Preamble:</u>

We, the people of Puerto Rico, in order to organize ourselves politically on a fully democratic basis, to promote the general welfare, and to secure for ourselves and our posterity the complete enjoyment of human rights, placing our trust in **Almighty God**, do ordain and establish this Constitution for the commonwealth which, in the exercise of our natural rights, we now create within our union with the United States of America.

Terminus:

... in the year of Our **Lord** one thousand nine hundred and fifty-two.

U.S. Virgin Islands - Organic Act
No mention.

- In almost all cases, states mention God in the preambles to their constitutions. Only a few do not. New Hampshire, Vermont, and Virginia do not have preambles. Tennessee's only mentions "Lord" in the context of dates. Oregon's preamble is decidedly neutral.
- The use of the term "in the year of our Lord" is very common.
- Many states mention God in sections that refer to religious freedom, but many of those refer to "Almighty God," which, by all objective standards, is an endorsement of the Judeo-Christian-Islamic deity (several of the religious freedom sections mention Christianity specifically).
- A handful of states have provisions that deny elective office to anyone who does not believe in God.
- The oaths of office codified in the various constitutions often include the closing statement, "So help me God." Several

149

states allow an alternate statement such as "Under the pains and penalties of perjury." Several do not allow an alternate closing, and several have no such closing whatever.

•

* us constitution.net

A few words from our
Presidents on the day of
their Inaugurations

1. George Washington- First Inaugural Address

it would be peculiarly improper to omit in this first official act my fervent supplications to that Almighty Being who rules over the universe, who presides in the councils of nations, and whose providential aids can supply every human defect, that His benediction may consecrate to the liberties and happiness of the people of the United States a Government instituted by themselves for these essential purposes, and may enable every instrument employed in its administration to execute with success the functions allotted to his charge

since we ought to be no less persuaded that the propitious smiles of Heaven can never be expected on a nation that disregards the eternal rules of order and right which Heaven itself has ordained; and since the preservation of the sacred fire of liberty and the destiny of the republican model of government are justly considered, perhaps, as *deeply*

Must accordingly pray that the pecuniary estimates for the station in which I am placed May during my continuance in it be limited to such actual expenditures as the public good may be thought to require

George Washington- 2nd Inaugural Address
No reference to God

2. John Adams-Inaugural Address

Relying, however, on the purity of their intentions, the justice of their cause, and the integrity and intelligence of the people, under an overruling Providence which had so signally protected this country from the first, the representatives of this nation, then consisting of little more than half its present number, not only broke to pieces the chains which were forging and the rod of iron that was lifted up, but frankly cut asunder the ties which had bound them, and launched into an ocean of uncertainty

155

if elevated ideas of the high destinies of this country and of my own duties toward it, founded on a knowledge of the moral principles and intellectual improvements of the people deeply engraven on my mind in early life, and not obscured but exalted by experience and age; and, with humble reverence, I feel it to be my duty to add, if a veneration for the religion of a people who profess and call themselves Christians, and a fixed resolution to consider a decent respect

3. Tomas Jefferson-First Inaugural Address

1st mention- Or have we found angels in the forms of kings to govern him? Let history answer this question.

2nd- enlightened by a benign religion, professed, indeed, and practiced in various forms, yet all of them inculcating honesty, truth, temperance, gratitude, and the love of man; acknowledging and adoring an overruling Providence, which by all its dispensations proves that it delights in the happiness of man here and his greater happiness hereafter—with all these blessings, what more is necessary to make us a happy and a prosperous people?

3rd- And may that Infinite Power which rules the destinies of the universe lead our councils to what is best, and give them a favorable issue for your peace and prosperity.

Tomas Jefferson-Second Inaugural Address

I shall need, too, the favor of that Being in whose hands we are, who led our fathers, as Israel of old, from their native land and planted them in a country flowing with all the necessaries and comforts of life; who has covered our infancy with His providence and our riper years with His wisdom and power, and to whose goodness I ask you to join in supplications with me that He will so enlighten the minds of your servants, guide their councils, and prosper their measures that whatsoever they do shall result in your good, and shall secure to you the peace, friendship, and approbation of all nations.

4. James Madison's 1st inaugural address

UNWILLING to depart from examples of the most **revered authority**, I avail myself of the occasion now presented to express the profound impression made on me by the call of my country to the station to the duties of which I am about to pledge myself by the most solemn of sanctions.

In these my confidence will under every difficulty be best placed, next to that which we have all been encouraged to feel in the guardianship and guidance of that **Almighty Being** whose power regulates the destiny of nations, whose blessings have been so conspicuously dispensed to this rising Republic, and to whom we are bound to address our devout gratitude for the past, as well as our fervent supplications and best hopes for the future.

2nd inaugural address

From the weight and magnitude now belonging to it I should be compelled to shrink if I had less reliance on the support of an enlightened and generous people, and felt less deeply a conviction that the war with a powerful nation, which forms so prominent a feature in our situation, is stamped with that justice which invites the **smiles of Heaven** on the means of conducting it to a successful termination.

Not to contend for such a stake is to surrender our equality with other powers on the element common to all and to violate the **sacred title** which every member of the society has to its protection.

5. James Monroe-First Inaugural Address

I enter on the trust to which I have been called by the suffrages of my fellow-citizens with my fervent prayers to the Almighty that He will be graciously pleased to continue to us that protection which He has already so conspicuously displayed in our favor

James Monroe- 2nd Inaugural Address

With full confidence in the continuance of that candor and generous indulgence from my fellow-citizens at large which I have heretofore experienced, and with a firm reliance on the protection of Almighty God, I shall forthwith commence the duties of the high trust to which you have called men for Christianity among the best recommendations for the public service, can enable me in any degree to comply with your wishes, it shall be my strenuous endeavor that this sagacious injunction of the two Houses shall not be without effect.

And may that Being who is supreme over all, the Patron of Order, the Fountain of Justice, and the Protector in all ages of the world of virtuous liberty, continue His blessing upon this nation and its Government and give it all possible success and duration consistent with the ends of His providence.

Caption on stamp: John Quincy Adams 1825-1829 · USA 22

6. John Quincy Adams- Inaugural Address

I shall look for whatever success may attend my public service; and knowing that "except the Lord keep the city the watchman waketh but in vain," with fervent supplications for His favor, to His overruling providence I commit with humble but fearless confidence my own fate and the future destinies of my country.

7. Andrew Jackson- First Inaugural Address

A diffidence, perhaps too just, in my own qualifications will teach me to look with reverence to the examples of public virtue left by my illustrious predecessors, and with veneration to the lights that flow from the mind that founded and the mind that reformed our system. The same diffidence induces me to hope for instruction and aid from the coordinate branches of the Government, and for the indulgence and support of my fellow-citizens generally. And a firm reliance on the goodness of that Power whose providence mercifully protected our national infancy, and has since upheld our liberties in various vicissitudes, encourages me to offer up my ardent supplications that He will continue to make our beloved country the object of His divine care and gracious benediction.

Andrew Jackson-2nd Inaugural Address

Finally,[2] it is my most fervent prayer to that Almighty Being before whom I now stand, and who has kept us in His hands from the infancy of our Republic to the present day, that He will so overrule all my intentions and actions and inspire the hearts of my fellow-citizens that we may be preserved from dangers of all kinds and continue forever a united and happy people.

8. Martin Van Buren-Inaugural Address

"...did I not permit myself humbly to hope for the sustaining support of an ever-watchful and beneficent Providence."

"This provident forecast has been verified by time."

"But to me, my fellow-citizens, looking forward to the far-distant future with ardent prayers and confiding hopes, this retrospect presents a ground for still deeper delight."

"Looking back to it as a sacred instrument carefully and not easily framed; remembering that it was throughout a work of concession and compromise; viewing it as limited to national objects; regarding it as leaving to the people and the States all power not explicitly parted with, I shall endeavor to preserve, protect, and defend it by anxiously referring to its provision for direction in every action."

"Beyond that I only look to the gracious protection of the Divine Being whose strengthening support I humbly solicit, and whom I fervently pray to look down upon us all. May it be among the dispensations of His providence to bless our beloved country with honors and with length of days.

9. William Henry Harrison-Inaugural Address

"I too well understand the dangerous temptations to which I shall be exposed from the magnitude of the power which it has been the pleasure of the people to commit to my hands not to place my chief confidence upon the aid of that Almighty Power which has hitherto protected me and enabled me to bring to favorable issues other important but still greatly inferior trusts heretofore confided to me by my country."

"We admit of no government by divine right, believing that so far as power is concerned the Beneficent Creator has made no distinction amongst men; that all are upon an equality, and that the only legitimate right to govern is an express grant of power from the governed." "He claims them because he is himself a man, fashioned by the same Almighty hand as the rest of his species and entitled to a full share of the blessings with which He has endowed them."

"a spirit which assumes the character and in times of great excitement imposes itself upon the people as the genuine spirit of freedom, and, like the false Christs whose coming was foretold by the Savior, seeks to, and were it possible would, impose upon the true and most faithful disciples of liberty."

"I deem the present occasion sufficiently important and solemn to justify me in expressing to my fellow-citizens a profound reverence for the Christian religion and a thorough conviction that sound morals, religious liberty, and a just sense of religious responsibility are essentially connected with all true and lasting happiness; and to that good Being who has blessed us by the gifts of civil and religious freedom, who watched over and prospered the labors of our fathers and has hitherto preserved to us institutions far exceeding in excellence those of any other people, let us unite in fervently commending every interest of our beloved country in all future time."

10. John Tyler-Inaugural Address

Tyler did not give a public inaugural address, but he does reference God in his speech accepting the office of president.

"While standing at the threshold of this great work he has by the dispensation of an all-wise Providence been removed from amongst us, and by the provisions of the Constitution the efforts to be directed to the accomplishing of this vitally important task have devolved upon myself."

"My earnest prayer shall be constantly addressed to the all-wise and all-powerful Being who made me, and by whose dispensation I am called to the high office of President of this Confederacy, understandingly to carry out the principles of that Constitution which I have sworn 'to protect, preserve, and defend.'"

"In conclusion I beg you to be assured that I shall exert myself to carry the foregoing principles into practice during my administration of the Government, and, confiding in the protecting care of an everwatchful and overruling Providence, it shall be my first and highest duty to preserve unimpaired the free institutions under which we live and transmit them to those who shall succeed me in their full force and vigor."

12. Zachary Taylor-Inaugural Address

On Monday March 5, 1849 President Taylor said "In the discharge of these duties my guide will be the Constitution , which I this day swear to "preserve, protect, and defend." For the interpretation of that instrument I shall look to the decisions of the judicial tribunals established by its authority and to the practice of the Government under the earlier Presidents, who had so large a share in its formation. To the example of those illustrious patriots I shall always defer with reverence, and especially to his example who was by so many titles "the Father of his Country." This right here proves that Zachary

Taylor wanted his leadership to be under God. Another religious fact about Zachary Taylor is that his inaugural address was suppose to be Sunday March 4, 1849 but he refused to do it on a Sunday so it was bumped to Monday.

13. Millard Fillmore-
He died before he could right his Inaugural Address.

14. Franklin Pierce-Inaugural Address

It must be felt that there is no national security but in the nation's humble, acknowledged dependence upon God and His overruling providence.

15. James Buchanan-Inaugural Address

" In entering upon this great office I must humbly invoke the God of our fathers for wisdom and firmness to execute its high and responsible duties in such a manner as to restore harmony and ancient friendship among the people of the several States and to preserve our free institutions throughout many generations."

" let me earnestly ask their powerful support in sustaining all just measures calculated to perpetuate these, the richest political blessings which Heaven has ever bestowed upon any nation."

"We ought to cultivate peace, commerce, and friendship with all nations, and this not merely as the best means of promoting our own material interests, but in a spirit of Christian benevolence toward our fellow-men, wherever their lot may be cast."

"I shall now proceed to take the oath prescribed by the Constitution, whilst humbly invoking the blessing of Divine Providence on this great people."

16. Abraham Lincoln's First Inaugural Address

"If the Almighty Ruler of Nations, with His eternal truth and justice, be on your side of the North, or on yours of the South, that truth and that justice will surely prevail by the judgment of this great tribunal of the American people."

Abraham Lincoln's Second Inaugural Address
"If we shall suppose that American slavery is one of those offenses which, in the providence of God, must needs come, but which, having continued through His appointed time, He now wills to remove, and that He gives to both North and South this terrible war as the woe due to those by whom the offense came, shall we discern therein any departure from those divine attributes which the believers in a living God always ascribe to Him?

17. Andrew Johnson-Inaugural Address
He did not have anything to say about God in his address.

18. Ulysses S. Grant – First Inaugural Address

"In conclusion I ask patient forbearance one toward another throughout the land, and a determined effort on the part of every citizen to do his share toward cementing a happy union; and I ask the prayers of the nation to Almighty God in behalf of this consummation."

Ulysses S. Grant – Second Inaugural Address.

"Why, it looks as though Providence had bestowed upon us a strong box in the precious metals locked up in the sterile mountains of the far West, and which we are now forging the key to unlock, to meet the very contingency that is now upon us."

"UNDER Providence I have been called a second time to act as Executive over this great nation. It has been my endeavor in the past to maintain all the laws, and, so far as lay in my power, to act for the best interests of the whole people."

19. Rutherford B. Hayes Inaugural Address

"Looking for the guidance of that Divine Hand by which the destinies of nations and individuals are shaped, I call upon you, Senators, Representatives, judges, fellow-citizens, here and everywhere, to unite with me in an earnest effort to secure to our country the blessings, not only of material prosperity, but of justice, peace, and union—a union depending not upon the constraint of force, but upon the loving devotion of a free people; "and that all things may be so ordered and settled upon the best and surest foundations that peace and happiness, truth and justice, religion and piety, may be established among us for all generations.'"

20. James A. Garfield-Inaugural address

With unquestioning devotion to the Union, with a patience and gentleness not born of fear, they have "followed the light as God gave them to see the light.

Let our people find a new meaning in the divine oracle which declares that "a little child shall lead them," for our own little children will soon control the destinies of the Republic.

They will surely bless their fathers and their fathers' God that the Union was preserved, that slavery was overthrown, and that both races were made equal before the law.

The Constitution guarantees absolute religious freedom. Congress is prohibited from making any law respecting an establishment of religion or prohibiting the free exercise thereof.

The Mormon Church not only offends the moral sense of manhood by sanctioning polygamy, but prevents the administration of justice through ordinary instrumentalities of law.

I shall greatly rely upon the wisdom and patriotism of Congress and of those who may share with me the responsibilities and duties of administration, and, above all, upon our efforts to promote the welfare of this great people and their Government I reverently invoke the support and blessings of Almighty God.

21. Chester A. Arthur-Inaugural Address

Summoned to these high duties and responsibilities and profoundly conscious of their magnitude and gravity, I assume the trust imposed by the Constitution, relying for aid on divine guidance and the virtue, patriotism, and intelligence of the American people.

22. Grover Cleveland-Inaugural Address

And let us not trust to human effort alone, but humbly acknowledging the power and goodness of Almighty God, who presides over the destiny of nations, and who has at all times been revealed in our country's history, let us invoke His aid and His blessings upon our labors.

23. Benjamin Harrison

*Entering thus solemnly into covenant with each other, we may reverently invoke and confidently expect the favor and help of **Almighty God**—that **He** will give to me wisdom, strength, and fidelity, and to our people a spirit of fraternity and a love of righteousness and peace.*

***God** has placed upon our head a diadem and has laid at our feet power and wealth beyond definition or calculation.*

24. Grover Cleveland

"I am sure my gratitude can make no better return than the pledge I now give before God and these witnesses of unreserved and <u>complete</u> devotion to the interests and welfare of those who have honored me."

"It cannot be doubted that our stupendous achievements as a people and our country's robust strength have given rise to heedlessness of those laws governing our national health which we can no more evade than human life can escape the laws of God and nature."

"Above all, I know there is a Supreme Being who rules the affairs of men and whose goodness and mercy have always followed the American people, and I know He will not turn from us now if we humbly and reverently seek His powerful aid."

25. William McKinley Inaugural address

I had searched for an inaugural address for the president and I could not find anything. So I'm not really sure if his speech referenced God or not

26.

In the inaugural address of **Theodore Roosevelt,** he (the president) refers to God as the Giver of Good, but he only mentioned him once throughout the entire speech. I am not entirely sure what sort of man Roosevelt was, and since I find it in poor taste to speak ill of the dead, I will assume that he was not a Christian, although he recognized God once.

27. William Howard Taft

I invoke the considerate sympathy and support of my fellow-citizens and the aid of the Almighty God in the discharge of my responsible duties.

28. Woodrow Wilson

1st Address:

The feelings with which we face this new age of right and opportunity sweep across our heartstrings like some air out of God's own presence, where justice and mercy are reconciled and the judge and the brother are one

God helping me, I will not fail them, if they will but counsel and sustain me!

2nd Address:

In their ardent heat we shall, in God's Providence, let us hope, be purged of faction and division, purified of the errant humors of party and of private interest, and shall stand forth in the days to come with a new dignity of national pride and spirit

I pray God I may be given the wisdom and the prudence to do my duty in the true spirit of this great people.

29. Warren G. Harding

Surely there must have been God's intent in the making of this new-world Republic

promote that brotherhood of mankind which must be God's highest conception of human relationship.

But with the realization comes the surge of high resolve, and there is reassurance in belief in the God-given destiny of our Republic. If I felt that there is to be sole responsibility in the Executive for the America of tomorrow I should shrink from the burden. But here are a hundred millions, with common concern and shared responsibility, answerable to God and country

I accept my part with single-mindedness of purpose and humility of spirit, and implore the favor and guidance of God in His Heaven. With these I am unafraid, and confidently face the future. 32 I have taken the solemn oath of office on that passage of Holy Writ wherein it is asked: "What doth the Lord require of thee but to do justly, and to love mercy, and to walk humbly with thy God?" This I plight to God and country.

30.Coolidge's Inaugural

Realizing that we can not live unto ourselves alone, we have contributed of our resources and our counsel to the relief of the suffering and the settlement of the disputes among the European nations. Because of what America is and what America has done, a firmer courage, a higher hope, inspires the heart of all humanity.

We stand at the opening of the one hundred and fiftieth year since our national consciousness first asserted itself by unmistakable action with an array of force. general cause of liberty we entered the Great War. When victory had been fully secured, we withdrew to our own shores unrecompensed save in the consciousness of duty done.

But if we wish to continue to be distinctively American, we must continue to make that term comprehensive enough to embrace the legitimate desires of a civilized and enlightened people determined in all their relations to pursue a conscientious and religious life.

Some never moved from their old positions, some are constantly slipping back to the old ways of thought and the old action of seizing a musket and relying on force.

. Peace will come when there is realization that only under a reign of law, based on righteousness and supported by the religious conviction of the brotherhood of man, can there be any hope of a complete and satisfying life. Parchment will fail, the sword will fail, it is only the spiritual nature of man that can be triumphant.

These rights and duties have been revealed, through the conscience of society, to have a divine sanction. The fundamental precept of liberty is toleration. We can not permit any inquisition either within or without the law or apply any religious test to the holding of office. The mind of America must be forever free.

The legions which she sends forth are armed, not with the sword, but with the cross. The higher state to which she seeks the allegiance of all mankind is not of human, but of divine origin. She cherishes no purpose save to merit the favor of Almighty God.

31. Herbert Hoover

It is a dedication and consecration under God to the highest office in service of our people. I assume this trust in the humility of knowledge that only through the guidance of Almighty Providence can I hope to discharge its ever-increasing burdens.

I ask the help of Almighty God in this service to my country to which you have called me.

32.President Franklin D. Roosevelt

"They concern, thank God, only material things."
1

"In this dedication of a Nation we humbly ask the blessing of God. May He protect each and every one of us. May He guide me in the days to come."2

Number of references to Deity in summary: 4

"They have no vision, and when there is no vision the people perish."3 (Proverbs 29:18 KJV)

"The money changers have fled from their high seats in the temple of our civilization."4 (John 2:13-17 KJV)

"While this duty rests upon me I shall do my utmost to speak their purpose and to do their will, seeking Divine guidance to help us each and every one to give light to them that sit in darkness and to guide our feet into the way of peace."5

"We of the Republic pledged ourselves to drive from the temple of our ancient faith those who had profaned it; to end by action, tireless and unafraid, the stagnation and despair of that day."6 (John 2:13-17)

"Shall we call this the promised land?"7 (Hebrews 11:9 KJV)

"We do not retreat. We are not content to stand still. As Americans, we go forward, in the service of our country, by the will of God."8

"For this we muster the spirit of America, and the faith of America."9

"As I stand here today, having taken the solemn oath of office in the presence of my fellow countrymen--in the presence of our God-- I know that it is America's purpose that we shall not fail."10
"The Almighty God has blessed our land in many ways. He has given our people stout hearts and strong arms with which to strike mighty blows for freedom and truth. given to our country a faith which has become the hope of all peoples in an anguished world."11
"So we pray to Him now for the vision to see our way clearly--to see the way that leads to a better life for ourselves and for all our fellow men--to the achievement of His will to peace on earth."

"...to the achievement of His will to peace on earth."12 (Luke 2:14 KJV)

33. Harry S. Truman

It is fitting, therefore, that we take this occasion to proclaim to the world the essential principles of the faith by which we live, and to declare our aims to all peoples.6 The American people stand firm in the faith which has inspired this Nation from the beginning. We believe that all men have a right to equal justice under law and equal opportunity to share in the common good. We believe that all men have the right to freedom of thought and expression. We believe that all men are created equal because they are created in the image of God.

From this faith we will not be moved.

People everywhere are coming to realize that what is involved is material well-being, human dignity, and the right to believe in and worship God.

But I say to all men, what we have achieved in liberty, we will surpass in greater liberty.69Steadfast in our faith in the Almighty, we will advance toward a world where man's freedom is secure.*70* To that end we will devote our strength, our resources, and our firmness of resolve. With God's help, the future of mankind will be assured in a world of justice, harmony, and peace.

34. Dwight d. Eisenhower:

First Inaugural address

MY friends, before I begin the expression of those thoughts that I deem appropriate to this moment, would you permit me the privilege of uttering a little private prayer of my own. And I ask that you bow your heads:

1

Almighty God, as we stand here at this moment my future associates in the executive branch of government join me in beseeching that Thou will make full and complete our dedication to the service of the people in this throng, and their fellow citizens everywhere.

2

Give us, we pray, the power to discern clearly right from wrong, and allow all our words and actions to be governed thereby, and by the laws of this land. Especially we pray that our concern shall be for all the people regardless of station, race, or calling.

3

May cooperation be permitted and be the mutual aim of those who, under the concepts of our Constitution, hold to differing political faiths; so that all may work for the good of our beloved country and Thy glory. Amen.

We are summoned by this honored and historic ceremony to witness more than the act of one citizen swearing his oath of service, in the presence of God

In our quest of understanding, we beseech God's guidance.

It establishes, beyond debate, those gifts of the Creator that are man's inalienable rights, and that make all men equal in His sight.

This is the work that awaits us all, to be done with bravery, with charity, and with prayer to Almighty God.

Second Inaugural address

Before all else, we seek, upon our common labor as a nation, the blessings of Almighty God

35. President John F. Kennedy

"For I have sworn before you and Almighty God
the same solemn oath our forebears
prescribed nearly a century and three quarters
ago."13
"And yet the same revolutionary beliefs for
which our forebears fought are still at issue
around the globe--the belief that the rights of
man come not from the generosity of the
state, but from the hand of God."14
"Finally, whether you are citizens of America or
citizens of the world, ask of us the same
high standards of strength and sacrifice which we
ask of you. With a good conscience our
only sure reward, with history the final judge of
our deeds, let us go forth to lead the land
we love, asking His blessing and His help, but
knowing that here on earth God's work
must truly be our own."15

"To those old allies whose cultural and spiritual
origins we share, we pledge the loyalty
of faithful friends."16
"Let both sides unite to heed in all corners of the
earth the command of Isaiah--to 'undo
the heavy burdens ... and to let the oppressed go
free.'"17 (Isaiah 58:7 KJV)

"Now the trumpet summons us again--not as a call to bear arms, though arms we need;
not as a call to battle, though embattled we are--but a call to bear the burden of a long
twilight struggle, year in and year out, "rejoicing in hope, patient in tribulation"--a
struggle against the common enemies of man: tyranny, poverty, disease, and war itself."18
(Romans 12:12 KJV)

36.Lyndon's Inaugural

My fellow countrymen, on this occasion, the oath I have taken before you and before God is not mine alone, but ours together.

Our destiny in the midst of change will rest on the unchanged character of our people, and on their faith.

They came here--the exile and the stranger, brave but frightened-- to find a place where a man could be his own man. They made a covenant with this land. Conceived in justice, written in liberty, bound in union, it was meant one day to inspire the hopes of all mankind; and it binds us still. If we keep its terms, we shall flourish.

The American covenant called on us to help show the way for the liberation of man. And that is today our goal. Thus, if as a nation there is much outside our control, as a people no stranger is outside our hope.

Change has brought new meaning to that old mission. We can never again stand aside, prideful in isolation. Terrific dangers and troubles that we once called "foreign" now constantly live among us. If American lives must end, and American treasure be spilled, in countries we barely know, that is the price that change has demanded of conviction and of our enduring covenant.

But we have no promise from God that our greatness will endure. We have been allowed by Him to seek greatness with the sweat of our hands and the strength of our spirit.

If we fail now, we shall have forgotten in abundance what we learned in hardship: that democracy rests on faith, that freedom asks more than it gives, and that the judgment of God is harshest on those who are most favored.

Each time, from the secret places of the American heart, came forth the faith they could not see or that they could not even imagine. It brought us victory. And it will again.

"Give me now wisdom and knowledge, that I may go out and come in before this people: for who can judge this thy people, that is so great?"

37. Richard Nixon

1st address
- What remains is to give life to what is in the law: to ensure at last that as all are born equal in dignity before God, all are born equal in dignity before man.
- I have taken an oath today <u>in the presence of **God**</u> and my countrymen to uphold and defend the Constitution of the United States. To that oath I now add this sacred commitment: I shall consecrate my office, my energies, and all the wisdom I can summon, to the cause of peace among nations.
- Only a few short weeks ago, we shared the glory of man's first sight of the world as **God** sees it, as a single sphere reflecting light in the darkness.

- A few short weeks ago, we shared the glory of man's first sight of the world as **God** sees it, as a single sphere reflecting light in the darkness.
- As the Apollo astronauts flew over the moon's gray surface on Christmas Eve, they spoke to us of the beauty of earth—and in that voice so clear across the lunar distance, we heard them invoke <u>**God's** blessing on its goodness.</u>
- "Let us go forward, <u>firm in our faith,</u> steadfast in our purpose, cautious of the dangers; but <u>sustained by our confidence in the will of</u> **God** <u>and the promise of man.</u>

2<u>nd</u> address

- <u>We shall answer to</u> **God,** to history, and to our conscience for the way in which we use these years.
- Today, I ask your prayers that in the years ahead <u>I may have</u> **God's** <u>help in making decisions that are right for America,</u> and I pray for your help so that together we may be worthy of our challenge.

197

- Let us go forward from here confident in hope, strong in our faith in one another, sustained by our faith in God who created us, and striving always to serve His purpose.

38. Gerald Rudolf Ford

References to God

1. But there is a higher Power, by whatever name we honor Him, who ordains not only righteousness but love, not only justice but mercy.

2. May God bless and comfort his wonderful wife and daughters, whose love and loyalty will forever be a shining legacy to all who bear the lonely burdens of the White House.

3. With all the strength and all the good sense I have gained from life, with all the confidence my family, my friends, and my dedicated staff impart to me, and with the good will of countless Americans I have encountered in recent visits to 40 States, I now solemnly reaffirm my promise I made to you last December 6: to uphold the Constitution, to do what is right as God gives me to see the right, and to do the very best I can f or America.

4. God helping me, I will not let you down.

References to Scripture

1. As we bind up the internal wounds of Watergate, more painful and more poisonous than those of foreign wars, let us restore the golden rule to our political process, and let brotherly love purge our hearts of suspicion and of hate.

References to Prayer

1. In the beginning, I asked you to pray for me. Before closing, I ask again your prayers, for Richard Nixon and for his family.

39. Jimmy Carter

I want to thank my predecessor for all he has done to heal our land.

we attest once again to the inner and spiritual strength of our Nation

the Bible used in the inauguration of our first President, in 1789, and I have just taken the oath of office on the Bible my mother gave me a few years ago, opened to a timeless admonition from the ancient prophet Micah:

3

"He hath showed thee, O man, what is good; and what doth the Lord require of thee, but to do justly, and to love mercy, and to walk humbly with thy God." (Micah 6:8)

—that we had remembered the words of Micah and renewed our search for humility, mercy, and justice.

40. RONALD REAGAN

1st Inaugural Address   In the eyes of many in the world, this every-4-year ceremony we accept as normal is nothing less than a miracle

Your dreams, your hopes, your goals are going to be the dreams, the hopes, and the goals of this administration, so help me God.

I am told that tens of thousands of prayer meetings are being held on this day, and for that I am deeply grateful. We are a nation under God, and I believe God intended for us to be free. It would be fitting and good, I think, if on each Inauguration Day in future years it should be declared a day of prayer.

with God's help, we can and will resolve the problems which now confront us.

God bless you, and thank you.

2nd Inaugural Address   God bless you and welcome back.

I wonder if we could all join in a moment of silent prayer. (Moment of silent prayer.) Amen.

When the first President, George Washington, placed his hand upon the Bible, he stood less than a single day's journey by horseback from raw, untamed wilderness

Well, with heart and hand, let us stand as one today: One people under God determined that our future shall be worthy of our past

My friends, together we can do this, and do it we must, so help me God.

There is no story more heartening in our history than the progress that we have made toward the "brotherhood of man" that God intended for us.

It is the American sound. It is hopeful, big-hearted, idealistic, daring, decent, and fair. That's our heritage; that is our song. We sing it still. For all our problems, our differences, we are together as of old, as we raise our voices to the God who is the Author of this most tender music. And may He continue to hold us close as we fill the world with our sound—sound in unity, affection, and love—one people under God, dedicated to the dream of freedom that He has placed in the human heart, called upon now to pass that dream on to a waiting and hopeful world.

God bless you and may God bless America.

41.George Bush "Our challenges are great, but our will is greater. And if our flaws are endless, God's love is truly boundless."

42. WILLIAM CINTON

1st Inaugural Address   When our founders boldly declared America's independence to the world and our purposes to the Almighty, they knew that America, to endure, would have to change

The scripture says, "And let us not be weary in well-doing, for in due season, we shall reap, if we faint not."

And now, each in our way, and with God's help, we must answer the call.

Thank you and God bless you all.

2nd Inaugural Address   Our rich texture of racial, religious and political diversity will be a Godsend in the 21st century. Great rewards will come to those who can live together, learn together, work together, forge new ties that bind together.

May God strengthen our hands for the good work ahead—and always, always bless our America.

43. George W. Bush

Ist Inaugural address

America, at its best, is compassionate. In the quiet of American conscience, we know that deep, persistent poverty is unworthy of our nation's promise. 28
And whatever our views of its cause, we can agree that children at risk are not at fault. Abandonment and abuse are not acts of God, they are failures of love.
And some needs and hurts are so deep they will only respond to a mentor's touch or a pastor's prayer. Church and charity, synagogue and mosque lend our communities their humanity, and they will have an honored place in our plans and in our laws.
I will live and lead by these principles: to advance my convictions with civility, to pursue the public interest with courage, to speak for greater justice and compassion, to call for responsibility and try to live it as well

God bless you all, and God bless America

<u>2nd Inaugurual address</u>

God moves and chooses as He wills

May God bless you, and may He watch over the United States of America

As I have read this addresses to our nation I would have to say that George W. Bush is a spiritual president and I believe he has stuck to the constitution and tried to keep this nation a Christian Nation.

44.   **Barack Obama** "Let it be said by our children's children that when we were tested we refused to let this journey end, that we did not turn back nor did we falter; and with eyes fixed on the horizon and God's grace upon us, we carried forth that great gift of freedom and delivered it safely to future generations."

Compiled by these students at Walk Right Bible
Institute for their class project:

Carissa Motes, Melissa Sutphin,
Hannah Burton, Josh White, Cody Williams, David
Pickle, Jen Marlowe, Valerie Holt, Jordan
Marowelli, Mary Dickson,
Heidi Hornbie, Morgan Peterson,
Aaron Tighe, Joe Anderson,
Jared Hill, Luke Miracle, John Hlatky, Shawn Rader,
Lindsay Patterson,
Michael Schnebelt, Camille Callen,
Emily Field, Brendan Wiltshire,
Becky Barnhard, Andrew Engle,
Stephanie Musick, Cody King,
Melody Spooner, Bethany Kilgore,
Alex Haymaker, Williesha Riddle,
Noeli Weinert.

The Boot Monument commemorates Major General Benedict Arnold's service and wounded foot at the Battle of Quebec and later his horse was shot out from under him at the Battle of Ridgefield. This monument recognizes his wounds in the Continental Army but contrives not to name him. Years later, after his traitorous betrayal of his country, Benedict Arnold met an American Officer in England and asked the officer what would happen to him if he returned to America. "We would cut off your leg and bury it with full military honors, and the rest of you we would hang."

ABOUT THE AUTHOR

Tim Schmig is a proud alumnus of Washington Elementary School in South St. Paul, MN. Blessed beyond all that he ever hoped for or expected, he is married to his High School Sweetheart- Sue Wallace of Lincoln Elementary School. The father of three beautiful daughters, he is affectionately known as "Papa" to four amazing grandchildren. Tim and Sue live in the historic Mason District of Owosso, Michigan in a Victorian home built in 1893 on the site of the old fairgrounds. His mission: tell the story of our unsung history.   timschmig@gmail.com

For Blake

Will we ever see the public profession of faith in our future documents? That all depends on who controls the narrative. As James Garfield said,

"Now more than ever the people are responsible for the character of their Congress. If that body be ignorant, reckless, and corrupt, it is because the people tolerate ignorance, recklessness, and corruption. If it be intelligent, brave, and pure, it is because the people demand these high qualities to represent them in the national legislature. . . . If the next centennial does not find us a great nation . . . it will be because those who represent the enterprise, the culture, and the morality of the nation do not aid in controlling the political forces."

Made in the USA
Columbia, SC
28 February 2023